401(K) & IRA

The Basics

YOUR LIFE, YOUR FUTURE
GET STARTED NOW

EDWARD T. O'BRIEN JR.

PAGE PUBLISHING, INC.
Conneaut Lake, PA

First originally published by Page Publishing 2020

This book was written for educational purposes only and is not intended as investment or tax advice. If investment or tax advice is needed, the services of a competent professional should be sought.

ISBN 978-1-64701-337-0 (pbk)
ISBN 978-1-64701-338-7 (digital)

Printed in the United States of America

Wishing you much success!

Best,

Ed

Dedication

This book is dedicated first to my wife, Sue, who has stood by my side and supported my endeavors through the many years of work, education and seclusion in the man cave for my research and writing. Second, with grateful acknowledgment to the many friends and former colleagues, who reviewed the drafts and provided helpful suggestions on the contents and flow. A special thanks to Mike, David, Sharon, and Bill, each of whom have been happily retired for several years with extensive personal experience in both corporate 401(k) plans and individual retirement accounts.

Finally, to the soldiers of Charlie Company, Second Battalion, 13th Infantry Regiment, my first active Army assignment and subsequent reassignment after my combat tour in Vietnam. This is where I grew into manhood, learned to take responsibility, and began my lifelong pursuit of higher education. The Platoon Sergeants and First Sergeants of Charlie Company threw every opportunity for training, classes, and leadership my way, and I dutifully accepted each one, which has made all the difference in my life. "Forty Rounds!"

Contents

Preface

Working for decades as an employee in corporate America, I watched my colleagues and other employees, including me, struggling to make sense of our employer-sponsored savings plans. I know and understand firsthand what employees are still going through today.

As I approached my fifth year in retirement, I felt it was the right time for me to share in brief book form what I learned on my long march to retirement. When I initially began saving in my employer's 401(k) plan, I had no idea what to invest in or how to manage my savings. I took a helter-skelter approach, investing in some of this and some of that, hoping my selections would grow to my benefit.

Back when my wife and I were dating, we began discussing our possible future together. We both worked for the same company at the time, which had a pension, but what was the possibility we'd be employed long enough to collect it? We'd also heard the never-ending concerns about the long-term viability of Social Security. So we decided early on to live on the larger of our after-tax paychecks and save the near equivalent of the other's after-tax amount. We did as well as we could with what we had and socked away the savings each payday.

After several years of contributing to our savings, a colleague happened to ask me what I knew about some options in our savings plan. I still had absolutely no idea, and when I thought about it that night, the ignorance I had about our investment options in the company plan didn't sit well with me.

This was our money that we were contributing to the savings plan every payday. Why didn't I know what it was we were investing in? Should we even be in the investments we were in? Was there anyone whom I could turn to and ask for guidance? My tech-savvy, intelligent colleagues obviously didn't know. Would my manager know?

So I asked my manager that very question. He told me that he'd only been investing in the company's stock and had been doing all right over the years. (The stock later collapsed. It recovered somewhat, but how did it affect my former manager when it fell? Was he retired at that time?)

After speaking with my manager back then, I was still left scratching my head. What about the other ten options we had available in our 401(k) plan, the ones where we had small amounts invested in each? Weren't they any good? Or could they be better than the company's stock?

Through the 1980s and early '90s, we were saving every payday. But I did not understand what we were investing in, and we weren't making much progress. I couldn't answer my colleague's question about the options in our plan. Heck, I couldn't even answer my own questions.

I had no one at work to turn to who had the knowledge to help me. We'd already been taken to the cleaners by an investment pro with our outside investments, which weren't much, but at the time, it was everything to us. Of course, this salesperson made his commission. But we lost every penny we'd been advised to invest, and in retrospect, the investment was totally unacceptable for our financial situation.

This is when I decided I'd had enough. It was time for me to take charge, to learn all I could about investing our personal savings and the tax effects on them, and then to explain it all to my wife as we went along.

It took me years of study, insurance and security licenses, professional certifications, and a graduate degree to put it all together. I even encouraged my wife to take a tax course so she could see the bigger picture. It's not how much you've saved but how much you get to keep.

Now I feel I must pass this information to you, to help you avoid the missteps and pitfalls I encountered along the way and the issues I've seen my clients undergo prior to their meeting with me. Certainly, you could research this information on the Internet yourself, as long as you know the topic or issue you're researching and the various nuances associated with it.

In this book, I lay it all out for you step-by-step, hand-holding you point by point, tax impact by tax impact; and I encourage you to seek additional information on your investments beyond the basics I will present to you. But you need to begin by knowing the basics.

If you have already started investing for your future, reading this book will help you to better understand the available options for growing and protecting your wealth. If you haven't yet begun investing for your future, then you should read this book and begin making your plans as soon as possible. The earlier you begin to save for your future, the longer you have time on your side working for you.

If you are looking forward to the day when you are completely in command of your time, financially set to do what you want, and can afford to do it, then this is the book to help you begin your journey. The information presented here is clear and straightforward. Don't worry about understanding all the options immediately, but use the information presented to ask questions that can help you choose the best options for you. Once you have grasped the general concepts and envisioned your successful outcome, you will become laser-focused.

Glossary of Terms

Please familiarize yourself with the following terms as I will refer to them in the chapters that follow.

actively managed funds—Actively managed funds, as opposed to indexed funds, comprise a basket of investments in various securities that attempt to outperform a stated benchmark by the management team. Active management comes with significantly higher fees than passive management. Investors in these funds hope the management will give them an edge over a comparative index, all costs considered. Let's just say that it sometimes happens, but more likely than not, it is very difficult to outperform the index for any length of time.

beneficiary forms—It is vitally important to execute a beneficiary form when opening any new account or after any life-altering event (marriage, divorce, remarriage, death, etc.). *Do not put this off.* Keep a copy of your beneficiary forms on file, listing the names, percentages, accounts, and so forth. Be sure the list is known to heirs and can be accessed for sharing with the attorney handling your estate.

bonds—Bonds are debt obligations that are issued by companies and municipalities to raise capital. The credit worthiness of a bond is reflected in its credit rating issued by recognized credit rating agencies. The percent of interest that it pays to bond holders is tied to its credit rating, length of time to the bond's maturity, and current Fed funds rate. Bonds are typically held by investors for current income or as a less volatile investment.

capital gains/losses—Special tax rates may be applicable to the gains or losses on your investments when sold, such as stocks, bonds, and mutual funds held in a taxable account and real estate investments. These can be short term (property held for one year or less) or long term (property held for longer than 365 days), filed with your annual tax return. Mutual funds held in a taxable account may throw off gains or losses annually when their portfolios are adjusted by the fund manager and will be reported to you (and the IRS) on a Form 1099.

Certified Financial Planner™—A CFP® is a financially experienced person who has completed at minimum a full year or longer course of study covering multiple areas of planning, passed an intensive multiday exam at the university level, and maintains annual continuing education requirements. One of the most important requirements for this practitioner is their absolute adherence to their fiduciary responsibilities to their clients.

compounding of interest—Compounding of interest is the effect, over time, of the reinvestment of interest (or dividends) within an investment that takes on a *snowball* effect (e.g., rolling a snowball down a mountain of snow, eventually becoming huge). The earlier you begin to save and reinvest, the lesser total money you will need to save to potentially end up with a much larger amount at some future date, say, retirement. If you start to save later in life, you will actually have to save much more at that time to compensate for the missed opportunity of the early years. *This is the power of compounding of interest.*

Note: In my tax preparation role, I prepared the return of a client who was receiving more than double her W-2 annual working salary in qualified company dividends alone. She had inherited stock from her mother, who had been reinvesting the dividends to purchase more shares in a company's stock for many, many years. Now the daughter was happily spending those dividends traveling the world.

enrolled agent—An enrolled agent (EA) is a person who has passed an intensive two-day exam given by the IRS and required annual continuing education. Once appointed as an EA, this person acts as a taxpayer advocate and is admitted to practice and represent the taxpayer before the IRS, with average fees typically lower than CPAs or attorneys.

ETFs (exchange-traded funds)—See the full description in the body of this document.

Fed funds rate—The Fed funds rate is the interest rate charged between banks for overnight loans and is used to control the supply of money.

index funds—Index funds are passively managed baskets of investments that track a stated benchmark, be that stock or bonds, with *substantially* lower fees than actively managed funds. In its simplest terms, passive management means that the fund manager or team assembles a portfolio of investments corresponding to the chosen benchmark and then goes on an extended coffee break.

laddered CDs—A number of CDs, usually three to five CDs, maturing each year and continually reinvested, if not withdrawn. To initiate, you purchase a one-year, two-year, three-year (four-year and five-year) CD. When each CD matures, you reinvest it for three to five years. You will then have one CD maturing each year, at nearly the highest available rates at the time of reinvestment, for as long as you continue to reinvest on maturity. And it is US government guaranteed too.

Here is a Standard & Poor's (S&P) example of a three-year ladder; a five-year ladder applies in the same manner.

Building a CD Ladder

Sample ladder strategy using staggered one-year maturities

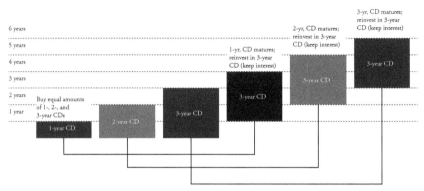

Source: ChartSource, Standard & Poor's Financial Communications. Example is hypothetical and assumes CDs are held to maturity. It is intended for illustrative purposes only and should not be construed as investment advice.

long-term assets—These are assets held for more than one year. Long-term assets currently receive favorable tax treatment if held in a taxable account.

mutual funds—See the full write-up description of mutual funds in the body of this document. Always, always, always check the fund's standard deviation and turnover ratio, found in the fund's prospectus, before investing.

rule of 72—This is a rule of thumb for how long it takes to double your money/investment. Divide 72 by the interest percentage to determine approximately how many years it will take to double the investment.

> The quickest way to double your money is to fold it in half and put it back in your pocket. (Unknown author)

securities—Securities are investments that are not guaranteed by the US government.

> They are not guaranteed, they are not secure,
> so naturally, the industry calls them securities.
> (paraphrased from Ed Slott)

short-term assets—These are assets held for less than one year. Unless considered "qualified" per the tax code, short-term assets held in a taxable account do not receive favorable tax treatment and are subject to taxes at your ordinary income tax rate. All dividends and all interest received during the year are short-term assets, even if reinvested in the same investment. If reinvested, it is referred to as *phantom income*, since you aren't directly taking hold of it in the hand. Certain dividends may qualify per the tax code to receive favorable "qualified dividends" tax treatment. If eligible, it will be so indicated on your annual 1099-B tax statement.

standard deviation—Standard deviation is a measurement of an investment's volatility. "Simply put, volatility is the range of price changes a security experiences over a given period of time. If the price stays relatively stable, the security has low volatility. A highly volatile security is one that hits new highs and lows, moves erratically, and experiences rapid increases and dramatic falls" (Investopedia).

stocks—Stocks are ownership of shares in a company's interests that are issued to raise capital at a lower cost to the company than debt. Stocks are priced and trade *today* at some perceived anticipated future multiple valuation or worth of the underlying company. Announcements, both positive and negative, will cause the price per share to swing in the market, sometimes wildly. Stocks are typically held by investors for capital appreciation and possibly dividend income.

stretch IRA—"A stretch IRA is an estate planning strategy that extends the tax-deferred status of an inherited IRA when it is passed to a non-spouse beneficiary. It allows for continued tax-deferred growth of an Individual Retirement Account (IRA). By using this strategy, an IRA can be passed on from generation to generation while beneficiaries enjoy tax-deferred and/or tax-free growth. The term 'stretch' does not represent a specific type of IRA; rather it is a financial strategy that allows people to stretch out the life—and therefore the tax advantages—of an IRA" (Investopedia). Google the SECURE Act for the recent Congressional changes to this former planning strategy.

turnover ratio—"The turnover ratio or turnover rate is the percentage of a mutual fund or other portfolio's holdings that have been replaced in a given year [calendar year or whatever 12-month period represents the fund's fiscal year]. The turnover ratio varies by the type of mutual fund, its investment objective and/or the portfolio manager's investing style. For example, a stock market index fund usually will have a low turnover rate, since it just duplicates a particular index, and the component companies in indexes don't change that often. But a bond fund will often have high turnover because active trading is an inherent quality of bond investments. Actively managed mutual funds with a low turnover ratio reflect a buy-and-hold investment strategy; those with high turnover ratios indicate an attempt to profit by a market-timing approach. An aggressive small-cap growth stock fund will generally experience higher turnover than a large-cap value stock fund" (Investopedia). Imperative that you read the full description at https://www.investopedia.com/terms/t/turnover-ratio.asp.

Introduction

Welcome to the first simplified basic primer on retirement investment planning that you will return to again and again and will gladly refer without hesitation to your coworkers, friends, children, and yes, even your parents. The explanations I provide in the following pages are based on my personal experience as well as working with colleagues and clients over many years. With this book, I intend to help you simplify your investing life and provide you with the knowledge you need to interact with your retirement savings plans.

The information contained in this book will help you avoid the hazards of investing in the wrong securities or aimlessly walking into a "gotcha!" tax trap. I will bring you quickly up to speed on the essentials necessary for you to actively participate in the retirement plans that are typically available to the average corporate employee while identifying many of the avoidable tax traps that people all too often trigger. Together, we will cut through the investment fog and make you comfortable with your retirement planning decisions.

Investment professionals are trained to help you reach your financial goals. For many people, reaching their goals requires the financial resources to enable participation in whatever money-dependent goal they may wish to pursue. Your goals may be national or world travel, a more expensive home, pursuit of additional education, providing for your children or grandchildren, supporting your charities, etc. As Mae West once said, "I've been rich and I've been poor, and rich is better."

I can't promise you that you'll become super rich, but the earlier you begin to participate with knowledge in your savings plans, the wealthier you will become. You'll certainly be doing a lot better for yourself financially after reading this book and getting inspired to take action.

Let's Get Started

Here's the opening question I have for you, and I'll bet I already know the answer. Has your company's HR department encouraged you to open a 401(k) in your company's retirement savings plan as one of your employment benefits, or have they opened it automatically for you upon hiring, as more companies are doing, only for you to then sit there blindly staring at your computer screen?

What about opening an online individual retirement plan with one of the major national investing firms? Still have that deer-in-the-headlights look about you?

Assuming you eventually got around to opening the plans, did you ask your coworkers what to invest in? And did they tell you, with a shrug of their shoulders, "Gee, I don't know, just pick something"?

Well, if that described your reaction to your retirement savings plans, we're about to have you exclaiming, "Wow! I wish I had known about this earlier. This is some great stuff!" Are you ready to get started?

In a recent online personal finance news article, it was stated that "four in 10 adults were only somewhat prepared for retirement, while 45% of adults in their fifties…are unprepared." It's not that people plan to fail; it's that people fail to plan. See https://www.fox-business.com/personal-finance/new-poll-americans-retirement.

We, you and I, are not going to let you end up as one of the 45% of older working adults who are financially unprepared to enter retirement. Together, we are going to change that. You are about to

21

take a gigantic leap from inaction into the planning phases of your financially secure retirement that will dramatically change your life.

When Will You Work with Financial Advisors?

When will you most likely find yourself engaging with an advisor? For most employees, it will occur when selecting investments in their IRAs, either during their working years or soon after retiring. You may also find yourself consulting with an advisor to select and allocate your 401(k) investment choices during your employment as you strategize to meet your goals.

Let's talk about your goals for a moment. Goals can be short term, in a few years from now, or as simple as a financially worry-free retirement in years to come. In other words, there are many goals in a person's life plan, all of which should be discussed, addressed, and understood when making important financially impacting decisions. Once made, plans often change, sometimes abruptly.

When this happens, you will need to seek the advice of a trusted advisor. You already know asking your coworkers for advice isn't going to be of much help (unless they've read this book). Furthermore, if you seek professional advice *after* you have made a financial transaction, it may be too late to avoid the tax consequences of your actions, which can be significant.

So before ever initially meeting with an advisor, you must have a basic knowledge of investments to ensure the complete comprehension of your conversation and subsequent actions taken with your advisor. That is what I wrote this book to do—to inform and educate you on the very basics of investing in your retirement plans and the tax consequences of those transactions.

Meeting with the Advisor

Never walk blindly into a meeting with a new advisor, because then you are totally at their mercy. Seek out references, ask questions, and get answers. Most importantly, be comfortable with the advisor at the end of the transaction.

Unless the advisor subscribes to and honors a fiduciary standard that holds *your* best interests in mind at all times, such as the *Code of Ethics* mandated by the Certified Financial Planner™ organization, there is always the risk that the advisor may only be looking after their own well-being. If you don't fully understand what it is you're investing in, *why would you want to invest in it?* In other words, don't get *sold* a product by some salesperson with a fancy title. *That's exactly what cleaned us out years ago.*

Instead, make your own decision to *buy* a product after considering the advice and guidance of a trusted advisor; know exactly what it is you are purchasing and how it fits into your plans. And make sure that it is the right product for you.

Advisor Fees

A short comment about advisors and their fees—advisors who work on an hourly basis are few, but they are out there. For a limited number of hours, they can work with you to establish your portfolio and then monitor it every so many months, perhaps twice a year, and certainly whenever abrupt things happen.

Otherwise, the majority of advisors are paid by commissions, specified fees, or both. Commissions are built into the sale of products. Fees can be structured as a percentage of *assets under management.*

If structured as assets under management, the advisor will want to manage a large portion of your investment portfolio for which they will charge you an annual fee, typically from 1%–2% of the assets under management. This fee may taper off to 1% or less as assets exceed $1,000,000.

The management fee may be negotiable, but it is not dependent on whether you have made a profit or sustained a loss. Of course, the manager will strive to create a profit for two reasons: first, to ensure earning their rising fee and keep you as a client, and second, hoping you will recommend them to others.

Radio host and financial advisor Dave Ramsey recommends using only front-end loaded funds. With front-end loads, the investor will only pay the advisor's fee once per investment transaction rather than the continual annual fees that are paid with an "assets under management" type of arrangement.

See https://www.daveramsey.com/blog/investing-fees-how-much-too-much.

In Dave's website example, an investment of $25,000, optimistically earning 10%–12% annually and held for thirty years, the results would appear as $500,000, $436,000, and $380,000, respectively per the annual advisory fees imposed.

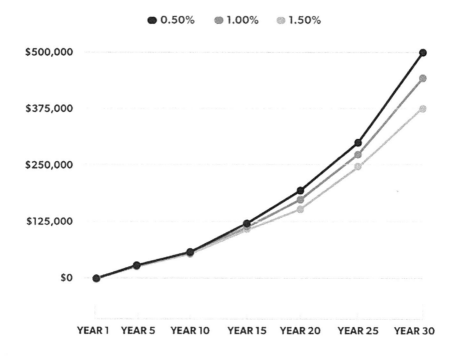

If you decide to use advisory services, I agree with Dave that using front-end loaded funds makes financial sense. Paying the advisor a one-time up-front fee compared to the annual advisory fees that continually eat away at an investment's growth can save you significant costs over the long term.

As you can see from the chart, ongoing advisory fees can eat into the growth of the investment; the lower the advisory fees paid out over time, the greater the potential growth of the investment. If seeking professional advice and ongoing assistance from a fiduciary, the up-front load appears to be the better and least costly choice for your portfolio over the long haul.

From personal experience, I was more than satisfied with the performance over time and the absence of ongoing advisory fees for the mutual funds I had inherited. The advisor, a CPA and eventual friend of my parents, who had been paid a front-end load when the funds were originally purchased, was always available to me for consultation. This is something for you to consider when investing in your IRAs.

Depending on your ability or desire to pay for services, you can select the method that best serves your needs. Or you can DIY and hope for the best results. Either way, this book will provide you with the basic knowledge for you to either work independently or with an advisor of your choosing to structure the investments that meet your personal plans and not the cookie-cutter approach that is used by too many firms today. See https://www.fidelity.com/viewpoints/personal-finance/financial-advisor-plan?ccsource=email_weekly.

Are Your Investments Guaranteed?

The only investments that are guaranteed are

- US government-insured and backed investments,
- bank accounts and certificates of deposit (CDs), and
- US government treasury bills, notes, and bonds.

If it doesn't say that it is guaranteed by the US government, then it is not guaranteed. Because of the guarantee, these investments offer some of the lowest rates of return to the investor.

Going beyond US government-guaranteed investments, you enter the uninsured world of investing and securities. There are some minimal guarantees, such as SIPC (Security Investors Protection Corporation), which guarantees you against the investing company taking your money and running off to the islands for endless mai tais. But that's about it for your investment protection. Be very careful of

Bernie Madoff-type *Ponzi* schemes. They're out there, and I know you've heard it before. If it sounds too good to be true, it probably is. Or as the Romans may have once said, "Caveat Emptor, Amica!"

Companies fail, go bankrupt, and cease to exist. Their underlying stock is declared worthless. You get $0 back.

Think bonds can't fail? Corporations go out of business and default on their bonds. City governments fail and default on their bonds. It happens.

Handling Risk / SWAN

In your initial meeting, investment professionals will typically ask you questions or provide you a questionnaire about your ability to take on risk. Mostly everyone is willing to take on some risks for increased reward, but most people are not willing to lose money! So be "eyes open" when responding to such questions.

If you can't sleep because of anxiety with your investment or the gyrating movement of the markets, then you are not helping yourself by remaining invested. You must understand time lines and the effects of business cycles on the markets and how it all affects the investment arena. Only then will you be able to SWAN (sleep well at night).

Investment values will change daily, sometimes significantly. The volatility in stocks—and yes, bonds—can be limited but cannot be totally controlled or eliminated. I see absolutely no need to invest in aggressive investments that have *roller-coaster* rides in the market when there are gentler *merry-go-round* type of investments that will work just as well for you in the long-term and not upset your stomach in the process. A well-diversified assortment of investments will help get you through the market cycles.

While you may not need a *budget* to live on—some people freak out when they hear that word—you should know where and how your income is spent. If you don't have a written record of your monthly expenditures, now would be a good time to begin one.

At the end of each month, I summarize our monthly expenses by category on an Excel spreadsheet, going through the checkbook and cash receipts. I even have a category line for savings, which I've continued since retiring. Not much goes into it now, as we're in the spend-down phase of life. While you're still in the accumulation phase of life, always pay yourself first (i.e., save) and then look to address the other categories of expenses.

But you *must* be able to identify where 95% of your income is going. Up to 5% can be relegated to the "I don't remember where I spent that or what I bought" category, but not more. If you can't identify 95% of your spending, you will need to dig until you can. See Appendix B for a list of the categories I use in my tracking sheet.

Let's talk for a moment about what I call the financial gap. The *financial gap* is the *difference* between the amount of guaranteed income you bring in monthly and your actual monthly spending. Guaranteed income includes Social Security retirement benefits, pensions, annuities, interest, dividends, etc.

During retirement, keep a sufficient amount of cash available that you can count on to cover your financial gap for no less than three years. Better still, if you can, reserve enough money to cover the gap for five to seven years *plus* a reasonable amount for a cost-of-living adjustment (COLA). Use laddered CDs, money market funds, and short-term bonds for this purpose, not stocks. You wouldn't want to have to sell at a loss to cover your gap needs in case of drastic market corrections or an extended recovery period.

The presidential candidates haven't a clue as to the price of a quart of milk. I do our grocery shopping several times weekly and know how the price of food has increased over time. Since retiring, groceries and medical costs have increased the most for us. We work the Internet to obtain the lowest hotel and airfare prices for our vacations, so consider including the COLA in figuring your spending, but don't be too frightened by it. Your investments should enable you to keep up.

Ensuring your financial gap is sufficiently covered will enable you to sleep well at night while your longer-term investments go through the market ups and downs.

Example:

Known monthly expenses:	<u>$6,000</u>
Guaranteed monthly income:	
Combined Social Security benefits	$3,000
Pension	$1,000
Dividends	$1,000
Interest	$350
Total recurring monthly income:	**<u>$5,350</u>**

Financial gap: $650/month

COLA @ 4%/ year
MMF @ 1.5%/ year
1-year CD @ 2% / 2-year CD @ 2.2% / 3-year CD @ 2.4% / 4-year CD @ 2.5%

Approximate amounts required to provide three to five years of SWAN gap coverage

Year 1	$7,700	(Keep in a **m**oney **m**arket **f**und and draw $650/month)
Year 2	$7,952	(Keep in a 1-year CD then move to the MMF, draw ~$676/month)
Year 3	$8,254	(Keep in a 2-year CD then move to the MMF, draw ~$703/month)
Year 4	$8,567	(Keep in a 3-year CD then move to the MMF, draw ~$731/month)

Year 5 $8,901   (Keep in a 4-year CD
                      then move to the MMF,
                      draw ~$760/month)

Financial gap coverage for three years requires approximately $23,906 to be set aside.
Financial gap coverage for five years requires approximately $41,374 to be set aside.

Laddered CDs providing the appropriate amount of anticipated annual gap coverage will give you restful, worry-free nights. Just make sure you have an adequate emergency fund set aside for those unexpected expenses we all run into. See the section on Roth IRA's for a great place to store your gap coverage CDs.

Individual And Employer Retirement Plans

This is where we begin to get into the meat of this book and examine the several ways for you to reach your financial goals using tax-advantaged accounts, including IRAs, Roth IRAs, 401(k) plans, and the investments in these accounts. This section is followed with a discussion of how immediate annuities may be used in an overall retirement financial plan.

The earlier you begin to invest, the wealthier you may become. One coworker around 1980 was telling me, "Ed, do you know that you can become a millionaire if you save $x each payday?" It sounded too good to be true, but it really is true. An average working person can save and, if properly invested, walk into their retirement without financial fear or anxiety.

I began saving when I was 18 and in the Army. The US government offered GIs stationed overseas a 10% interest savings plan. I immediately signed up, saving $10/month to begin with. I was only making $110/month before taxes, so this was a rather large deduction for a private back in 1966. Several years later, when needing to furnish our home, a nice, plump check arrived in the mail, which really helped with the purchase.

The key to building wealth is to not spend every dime you earn. Now let's get you pumped up and into action, beginning with IRAs.

Traditional IRAs

Individual Retirement Accounts (IRAs) are specified by law and outlined in IRS Publication 590. Once opened with banks or investment firms, these *traditional IRAs* enable any individual with earned income to contribute to their IRA in a tax-deferred basis.

Depending on a person's income level and whether they are covered by an employer's retirement plan, the contributions going into the account may be income tax deductible. If the contributions are not income tax deductible (i.e., the individual does not meet the qualifying requirements for deductibility), the individual may still make a *nondeductible* IRA contribution.

If you make a nondeductible contribution to your IRA, you must file IRS Form 8606 with your annual tax return in the year of the contribution. You submit this form with your annual tax return every year you make another nondeductible contribution. The Form 8606 tracks all nondeductible IRA contributions. Later, when making your retirement withdrawals from your IRA, you will again file the Form 8606 to avoid paying taxes twice on those nondeductible contributions.

There are contribution limits for IRAs. For example, in tax year 2019, if you were under age 50, you could contribute up to $6,000 or up to your maximum earned income, whichever is lower. If you were age 50 or over, you could also contribute an additional $1,000 annually, called a *catch-up* contribution, again subject to your maximum earned income. See example below. Over the years, Congress occasionally approves changes/increases to the annual retirement savings contribution limits.

To obtain the current information, do an online search for "[year] IRA contribution limits." The resulting search hits will illustrate the income limitations applicable for income tax deductibility and any changes to the contribution limits.

Example:

> Earned income = $5,000 (Your total IRA contri-
> bution is limited to $5,000.)
> Earned income = $20,000 (Your contribution
> maximum is $6,000 or $7,000 if age 50 or older.)

The key point here is that a person must have earned income to contribute to a Traditional IRA.

Financially speaking, the sooner you open and maximize your contributions, the better off your retirement years can be. Remember the power of compounding of interest. Contributions are income tax deductible if qualified, and all earnings grow tax-deferred until withdrawn (normally after age 59½).

Example:

> Begin saving $5,000/year for forty-two years
> (to age 65), beginning at age 23 when you're
> beginning your career, earning an average annual
> return of 7%. Ready? That's $1,153,161.
> How about if you max the current IRA limit of
> $6,000/year using the same parameters? Ready?
> That's $1,383,793.
> What if you procrastinate and don't start saving
> until ten years later, at age 33?
> Same parameters, with $5,000/year, that's
> $551,091.
> Same parameters, with $6,000/year, that's
> $661,309.

Either way is still a nice amount, but starting ten years earlier, at age 23, with only $50,000 or $60,000 additionally invested over the span of those years, results in more than doubling your projected growth amount by the time you retire. The results are clear—starting to save later leaves only two possible outcomes: (1) your savings won't grow as much as they could have had you started saving earlier, or (2) you will need to save more, probably much more, to reach the same results than if you had begun saving earlier.

Don't procrastinate any longer. Take charge and invest in your future.

You can play with more numbers at this website. See https://keisan.casio.com/exec/system/1234231998.

And yes, you may still open an IRA even if you have other retirement plan coverage, such as a 401(k) or similar employer-sponsored plan. If you can afford to do it, maximize your retirement savings at every opportunity. Got a 3% pay raise? Increase your savings by 1½% to 2%. Do this every year until you are maxing out your retirement opportunities. Live for today, but don't ignore your future.

Tip: If you have a personal business and have children in your family, you could hire them for various chores in the business and pay them a wage. That wage could then be used to fund their IRA.

Spousal IRAs

If you are married and only one spouse has earned income, you may also open and contribute to a spousal IRA for the spouse without the earned income. The same contribution amounts apply based on their age (i.e., age 50 and over for the *catch-up* contribution), and your earned income must be at least as much as your total combined IRA contributions.

Look further back on these pages for the numbers that could be possible if you both contributed to IRAs.

Getting excited yet?

Investing in an IRA

To invest in an IRA, contact or visit your local bank, credit union, CPA, CFP®, or any of the major investment firms (Schwab, Fidelity, Vanguard, TD Ameritrade, etc.). Fill out the application and submit at least the minimum amount required to open the account. Instruct the company to invest the money in one of their money market funds until you have researched your investment options. Then instruct the company to move the money from the money market fund by purchasing the investment you've selected (or do it yourself online once you're familiar with that process).

See the section on "Typical Investments Available in an Employer's 401(k) Plan" to help educate you on similar investments that may be available to you in your IRA. Also, keep in mind that IRAs enable you to invest in a plethora of securities, unlike the limited number found in the typical 401(k) plan.

Withdrawing from an IRA

To make withdrawals from your IRA, contact the investment institution administrator where your IRA is located and request the withdrawal. You may have the administrator withhold an amount for income tax or withdraw the full amount without withholding income tax. You will be asked by the administrator as to your preference for the tax (i.e., withhold or not withhold). The funds can be electronically transferred to your local bank account or sent to you in a check.

Withdrawals from IRAs will be subject to tax at your ordinary income tax rates. For convenience, I personally have my IRA administrator withhold the income tax from my withdrawals.

Withdrawals from IRAs made prior to age 59½, in most cases, will also be subject to a 10% penalty in addition to the income tax that is due. There are some qualifying breaks from the penalty for first-time home purchases, illnesses, etc., but very limited otherwise.

It is in your best interest not to withdraw from your IRA before retirement and especially before reaching retirement age. If you were to withdraw $50,000 from your IRA prior to age 59½ for nonqualifying reasons, you could be facing over $15,000 in federal taxes *and* penalties if you are in the 20% marginal tax bracket and reside in a state with no income tax. If your state of residence has an income tax and your marginal tax bracket is in the 24% range, it's even worse. You could be looking at a tax and penalty of nearly $21,000 from your retirement fund. That's a 42% hit to your pocket. And you *thought* you were in the 24% tax bracket.

Rollover IRAs

Rollover IRAs are generally former 401(k)s that have been rolled out to an IRA upon leaving the previous employment. As long as the money in the rollover IRA remains separate from any other IRA, it retains its IRS qualification and can be later rolled into the next employer's 401(k) plan (as long as the next employer's plan permits it). However, if the rollover IRA is comingled with an existing traditional IRA or added to with additional contributions, it loses its IRS qualification and negates the ability to roll it to the next employer.

RMD (Required Minimum Distributions)

As of this publication, beginning at age 72, an individual *must* begin withdrawing from their IRA per the schedule outlined in IRS Publication 590. This is called an RMD, a required minimum distribution. The Treasury and IRS have decided that you've had the taxes on your savings deferred long enough and that it's time to pay up. Google the SECURE Act for recent updates.

The RMD amount is based on the combined value of all your non-Roth IRA accounts as of December 31 of the preceding year. The withdrawal must be equal to or greater than the amount calculated per the IRS publication. You can always withdraw more money; however, if you underwithdraw (i.e., withdraw less than what was required per the RMD calculation), you will be in for a *50% penalty* on the amount that was not distributed.

For your first RMD, you have a choice to either withdraw your RMD in the same tax year you turn 72 or wait until April 1 of the year following the year when you turn 72. If you decide to wait until April 1 of the following year, you will be required to make two (2) RMD withdrawals in that tax year by December 31. From that point on, you must make your annual RMD every year by December 31.

The potential problem with delaying your first RMD withdrawal until April 1 of the year following the year when you turn 72 is that by taking two RMDs in the same tax year, you run the chance of pushing yourself into the next higher tax bracket. Think it through and discuss it with your tax advisor if necessary.

If you have more than one IRA (yes, you may have several, perhaps you've listed different beneficiaries on them), you can withdraw the total amount of your RMD from just one IRA or a smaller amount from each IRA, as long as you withdraw at least the entire amount required to be withdrawn. When I take my annual RMD, I have the administrator withdraw more than the calculated RMD amount from my money market fund and withhold it for taxes. I cover two birds with one transaction—meeting my annual RMD and paying my tax bill.

Roth IRAs

Roth IRAs are one of the more recent twists to retirement savings. *Contributions* to Roth IRAs are made with *after-tax dollars*, and there are no current income tax savings. Earnings grow tax-free and are withdrawn tax-free as long as the account has been opened for at least five years and the person is age 59½ or older upon withdrawing. *Both rules must be met.*

The initial opening date of the Roth IRA begins the five-year clock, and all subsequent annual contributions assume the date of the initial contribution that opened the account. Since the initial opening date is considered to be the *tax year* the Roth IRA is first opened, technically holding for four calendar years and a couple of days meets the *five-year* rule.

A person may open and contribute to a Roth IRA in addition to a traditional IRA, but only up to a set maximum amount of money per year. You may contribute all to one, all to the other, or split between the two; but you may only contribute up to the legally permissible maximum annual amount.

Original contribution amounts to Roth IRAs are always available for withdrawal by the account owner at any time without income tax, since they were funded with after-tax dollars. All *earnings* must qualify per the five-year and age 59½ or older rules, or they will be subject to a 10% penalty and income tax, regardless of your age.

There are no RMD requirements for Roth IRAs. There is also no age contribution limit. *You must have earned income to make a contribution*, and if you are still working at age 100 (and within the earnings limits), you can make a contribution.

Remember the example about the growth of money in an IRA? *Now imagine it tax-free!*

Conversion to a Roth IRA

If you want a Roth IRA but were precluded from directly contributing to one because your annual income was too high, there is a work-around. You have the ability to "back door" a Roth IRA by making a *conversion* to a Roth IRA from a traditional or rollover IRA.

Conversion to Roth IRAs from traditional or rollover IRAs can be made by working with your savings institution to convert an amount of dollars (or a number of shares equivalent to an amount of dollars) to a Roth IRA at any time, whether you are still working or retired and not bringing in an earned income. A conversion in the tax code is treated the same as a withdrawal, so you must pay income tax on the amount that is converted in the conversion tax year.

I would not recommend converting to a Roth IRA when you are in a high-income tax bracket. Better to wait until you are retired and in a lower income tax bracket to make the conversion.

Converting when you are in a lower tax bracket is a great gift to you by Congress. Assuming you earned the money to contribute to your original IRA while in the 25% or higher tax bracket, and possibly having even gotten a tax break on your earlier contributions, you now convert to the Roth IRA and pay taxes in the lower tax brackets on the amount converted. That's a sweet deal by anyone's standards.

You will have to pay income taxes at your then current income tax rate on the amount of the conversion. In your working years, income taxes are automatically withheld from your paycheck. In this case, you may need to submit a Quarterly Estimated Tax payment to the IRS using Form 1040-ES at the time of the conversion to avoid any late payment penalties, unless you have your annual taxes covered sufficiently by other means.

Once converted, the conversion and any earnings will grow tax-free as long as they qualify under a *separate* five-year rule. Each and every conversion will take on a new separate five-year holding period. Converted amounts are always available to you, since you will have paid the income tax when you made the conversion. However, all *earnings* for that conversion will run with each new five-year clock before they can be withdrawn tax-free.

Final notes about conversions to Roth IRAs: If you are subject to the RMD (i.e., you are over 72 years of age), you must first take your annual RMD before doing any conversion to the Roth IRA. If you convert before taking your RMD, you will have walked into a world of tax hurt. Do your RMD first; make your conversion second. Lastly, if you are converting to a Roth IRA from an IRA that was funded or partially funded earlier with nondeductible contributions, you will need to submit a Form 8606 when completing your federal tax return for that tax year.

Which IRA Should You Choose— Traditional IRA or Roth IRA?

Which IRA you choose depends on whether you need current income tax relief or want your savings to be later withdrawn tax-free. The recommendation in financial circles is that younger workers will be better off if they go with the Roth IRA and forego the current income tax deductibility, since no one knows what future regular tax rates will be (applicable to withdrawals from traditional IRAs and 401(k)s). Perhaps investing in some of each type of IRA is an idea, especially if you need a current tax break now and qualify for the deduction available with a traditional IRA but still want to hedge against future income tax increases.

Roth IRA contributions are also limited by annual income. Your ability to contribute to it is phased out as income levels rise. Of course, if you do not qualify for a current tax break with a traditional

IRA but your annual income is within the range to contribute to a Roth IRA, then you have your answer right there.

You have until April 15 to make your IRA contributions for the previous tax year, be it traditional (deductible or nondeductible), Roth, or spousal. Don't let that date slip past you.

Creating a Roth IRA to Use as Your "Never Taxed" Emergency Fund

You've heard this before, during your working years, keep at least six months of income available in your *emergency fund*. I imagine that there are a lot of government employees who are working on building their emergency funds after being unfortunately and unsuspectingly cut out of their normally guaranteed paychecks for several months during the 2018–19 federal budget exercise.

Since a Roth IRA is funded with after-tax dollars, you may withdraw your contributions at any time without additional tax or penalties. Do not withdraw any earnings if you have not passed the time and age qualification requirements because those earnings will be subjected to tax and penalty. However, the contribution amounts that you made are always available to you.

If you save your emergency fund in a taxable bank account, as most people would likely do, you'll pay taxes on the interest—every year. If you save your emergency fund in a taxable money market fund or account or a taxable CD, you'll pay taxes on the interest—every year.

But if you move your money from *taxable account A* to *never-taxed account B*, you'll never pay taxes on the qualified earnings! What better means do you have at your disposal than to build up another retirement plan, not have to be concerned about paying taxes every year on your earnings, and have money available to you in case of dire need? I just wish I could have spoken to those government employees before they were run over by the political bus.

With a Roth IRA, your contributions are always available for you to withdraw if you need to use them, and the earnings grow tax-free once qualified. It doesn't get any better than this to create and grow your emergency fund. To quote Ed Slott, "Go from forever taxed to never taxed."

For your six-month emergency fund requirements, consider directing your contributions into your money market accounts or money market fund and short-term CDs. All of which are in your tax-free accounts, of course. Once you have your emergency fund requirements adequately covered, direct your future Roth IRA contributions into the longer-term retirement investments.

If you find it necessary to tap your Roth IRA *emergency* fund, only withdraw the amount that you actually need. If you need more, go back for another bite of the apple, but if you initially withdraw more than you need, you will not be able to redeposit it. Preserve as much as you can in the Roth account.

401(k) Plans (Traditional and Roth)

The *401(k) plans* are employment-sponsored retirement plans where employees make tax-deductible contributions to save for their future retirement. Many 401(k) plans receive matching contributions of some percent by the employer for up to a specified amount of the employee's contributions, and some companies will also make profit sharing contributions.

Don't pass up this opportunity to grow your wealth with free money! At the very least, contribute enough to your 401(k) to obtain the maximum amount of employer contributions to your savings. More if you can, certainly, but at least the amount necessary to obtain the maximum amount of free money.

The 401(k) plans take their name from the tax code authorizing an employer to provide this *qualified* retirement savings plan to their employees. Qualified retirement plans receive special treatment per the tax code. Among other things, the special treatment includes the ability to defer taxes on large amounts of your annual compensation, move your savings from employer to employer when changing jobs, take loans from your savings (must be repaid or it is considered a withdrawal), and withdraw sums without penalty when retired and aged 55 or over.

The 401(k) plans were implemented as businesses began eliminating employer-provided and paid pensions for their employees, thus putting the burden of financial security during retirement fully on the backs of the employees. It is what it is, so a person should make the best of the situation and fund their 401(k), at least to the minimal amount necessary to receive the maximum company matching contributions to the plan, if such matching contributions are provided by the employer. Of course, maximizing your annual contributions to the legal limit (which has been raised over the years) is a good stretch objective.

Contribution Limits

For tax year 2019, individuals who are under age 50 may contribute up to $19,000 of their earned income to their 401(k) plan. If age 50 or over, you may also contribute an additional $6,000 annually, called the *catch-up* contribution, for a total of $25,000 each year. Over the years, Congress occasionally approves changes/increases to the annual retirement savings contribution limits. To find the current 401(k) plan contribution limits, perform an online search for "[year] 401(k) contribution limits."

Example of a traditional 401(k) plan annual savings:

Let's say you're earning $75,000 gross income, and you begin to save 15% of your gross pretax in your employer's traditional 401(k) plan. That amounts to $11,250/year. Since the savings contribution reduces your gross income, you'll only pay income taxes on the lower gross of $63,750.

When you factor in how the tax savings applicable to your lower gross income applies to the overall equation, your 15% savings amounts to only a 13% reduction to your total net income. If you boost your savings to 20% of gross income in the traditional 401(k), considering the tax off-set, you'll only reduce your total net income by approximately 17%.

As you can tell, I like round numbers, numbers that end in 0 or 5 with a 1 or a 2 in front of them. So 15% would be my recommended minimum savings to start with, going for 20% with the next or, at most, two pay raises. Try it and see how you manage your finances. If you absolutely can't tolerate the 15%, then back it down to 10% until the next pay raise. Don't put it off.

If you are focused on your goals, you can certainly trim your spending to enable you to maximize your savings. Force yourself to begin at the 15% savings rate, and from that point forward, contribute half of each raise or bonus you receive to your 401(k) until you have maxed it out, looking forward to your financially comfortable retirement years.

The 401(k) contributions are income tax deductible on your current annual earnings. All contributions and earnings grow tax-deferred until withdrawn. That is the good side of 401(k) plans.

Unfortunately, most plans do not come with expert advice to hand-hold and guide the employee in creating, monitoring, and adjusting their plan. That is where this book attempts to help you understand how to engage and interact with your company's plan.

Typical Investments Available in an Employer's 401(k) Plan

Company benefit administrators, usually in your HR department, work with investment companies to create a selection of various mutual funds for their 401(k) plan. These will usually be a variety of indexed mutual funds composed of stocks and/or bonds with very low ongoing management fees.

Moving higher up the mutual fund management fee scale structure are combinations of stocks and bonds, growth or value stock funds, several target-date specific trusts, and usually on the highest end of management fees, the international stocks and/or bonds. You will also have at least one money market fund with the lowest of management fees. There may also be, but not always, an investment selection in the shares of the employer's stock.

Let's examine a few of the more popular 401(k) plan investment categories available to employees, acknowledging the partial use of Vanguard investments' online descriptions in several of the following:

Large-cap index funds. A large-cap index fund is a passively managed fund providing a breadth of large-capitalization equity exposure (i.e., the top 4/5 of the largest companies). Aside from the general stock market volatility, these funds' main risk comes from investing only in the stocks of large US companies when other market segments (e.g., mid-cap, small-cap, international) may be outperforming. These funds are suitable for *long-term* investors seeking exposure to the largest US stocks.

Mid-cap index funds. A mid-cap index fund is a passively managed fund providing a breadth of mid-capitalization equity exposure (i.e., in medium-sized companies). Mid-caps can be more volatile than larger companies, and that is a key risk to consider. Your portfolio *should be diversified* before venturing into this type of fund.

Small-cap index funds. A small-cap index fund is a passively managed fund providing a breadth of small-capitalization equity exposure (i.e., in smaller-sized companies). The primary risk in small-cap funds is their investment in a highly volatile section of the market. Your portfolio *should be well-diversified* before considering venturing into an aggressive fund of this type, and you should expect to see a wide standard deviation as well.

Bond funds. Bond funds can help add stability to your portfolio when included in a well-balanced portfolio and help balance the risks associated with stock funds. By potentially holding hundreds—sometimes thousands—of bonds in a single fund, you get more diversification than you would buying individual bonds. Bond mutual funds give your portfolio the opportunity to earn income, unlike money market funds, which focus on protecting your cash.

Balanced funds. Balanced funds are typically structured as a low-cost, broadly diversified index fund offering investors an easy way to gain exposure to both stocks and bonds. This type of fund strives to maintain an investment of roughly 60% in stocks and 40% in bonds by tracking the indexes representing broad barometers of the US equity and US taxable bond markets. Certain retirement trust funds invert the stock/bond balance allocation by investing 60% in bonds and 40% in stocks. Investors with a *long-term* time horizon who want growth and some income, or income and some growth—and who are willing to accept stock and bond market volatility—may wish to consider these types of funds as *core* holdings in their portfolio.

Growth funds. A growth fund invests in stocks of large US companies in market sectors that tend to grow more quickly than the broader market. A low-cost growth index fund follows a buy-and-hold approach and invests in substantially all the stocks represented in its broad benchmark. The fund's primary risk, apart from general stock market volatility, comes from the fact that its focus on large-capitalization growth stocks may, at times, underperform the broader stock market.

Value funds. A value fund invests in stocks of large US companies in market sectors that tend to grow at a slower pace than the broader market; these stocks may be temporarily undervalued by investors. A low-cost value index fund follows a buy-and-hold approach and invests in substantially all the stocks contained within its broad benchmark. In addition to general stock market volatility, the fund's primary risk comes from the fact that, at times, its focus on large-capitalization value stocks may underperform the broader stock market.

Target date trusts. Target date trusts offer a broadly diversified portfolio. Each target date trust invests in several low-cost index funds to create a broadly diversified mix of stocks and bonds. The year in a target date trust's name is its target date, the approximate year in which an investor in the trust expects to retire and leave the workforce.

Target date trusts will automatically adjust investments over time. A target retirement trust will hold more stocks the further away it is from its target date, seeking stocks' higher potential growth. Stocks also have the highest risk of loss. To reduce risk as the target date approaches, investment managers will gradually decrease the trust's stock holdings and increase its bond holdings. Bonds usually have a lower risk of loss, though they also have lower potential gains.

Target date trusts can be very good for planning purposes leading to your retirement and beyond. However, you need to take extra caution when investing in target date trusts, as not all such trusts operate in the same manner. You will need to know *when the trust will begin switching* to a more conservative position by holding increasingly larger amounts of bonds and cash from their initial majority stock positions.

Some trusts begin switching investments in advance of the specified target date and are conservatively set upon reaching the target date or soon thereafter. Other trusts will only begin switching upon reaching the target date and then take upward of thirty or more years to reach their most conservative investing position.

During the 2008 market meltdown, retirees in many 2000/05/10/15 target date trusts were shocked to learn their trusts were still predominantly invested in equities while their account values shrank. As long as you are aware of when a target date trust begins to move into more conservative investments and the length of time it takes them to reach their most conservative position—information that should be stated in the fund's prospectus—you can confidently invest in and adjust the percentage of your investments across several such trusts as you wish.

International stock and/or bond funds. These funds offer investors low cost ways to gain equity or bond exposure to both developed and emerging international economies. The funds track stock or bond markets all over the globe, *with the exception of the United States.* Because these funds invest in non-US stocks or bonds, including those in developed and emerging markets, the funds can be more volatile than similar domestic funds. Long-term investors who want to add a diversified international equity or bond position to their portfolio may want to consider these funds as options. If you absolutely have to reach beyond the US markets, it is advisable to invest no more than 5% of your savings in any type of international fund, stock or bond.

Stable value funds. A stable value fund, also known as a money market fund (MMF), seeks to *preserve* the cash principal and produce positive returns that move in the general direction of market interest rates. The fund is designed to have lower volatility than most bond funds and will typically return interest that is closely comparable to a six-month or one-year CD rate, although it is not guaranteed by the US government.

Continuous allocation of 5%–10% of the total paycheck contributions to your 401(k) plan and directed into the stable value fund would be advisable to build up a nice cash balance for you over time. This large cash bundle may later be redirected into other investments in your plan on major market corrections.

Company stock funds. Employees wishing to participate in the market progress of their employer may have an opportunity to invest in company stock in their plan. Since this will be a one-stock investment, it should be considered as the most aggressive and the riskiest investment that you can make in your 401(k) plan.

Generally speaking, a person may not want to invest in the same company from where they draw their paycheck, as the risk of losing both one's savings and one's employment are ever present. If you decide to include your employer's stock as one of your 401(k) investments, it is advisable to limit such amount to no more than 10% of your investment total.

Withdrawing from a 401(k) is normally considered and taxed as ordinary income. However, in certain circumstances, you may be able to treat the employer's stock in your 401(k) as a capital gain instead of ordinary income. If so and eligible for what is known as *net unrealized appreciation,* the capital gains tax rates may provide a more favorable tax treatment for this particular investment. Work with your tax advisor and financial advisor to see if this pertains to your particular situation, and choose the lower tax option.

Self-directed IRA. Some 401(k) plans offer to participants the ability to move majority of their 401(k) savings to a self-directed IRA. If your plan offers this feature, you have, in my opinion, struck the *gold mine* of 401(k) plans. Once you have established your self-directed IRA with the servicing financial institution, you can easily move funds back and forth between your 401(k) and the IRA using each account's money market fund.

An IRA provides the investor a plethora of investments and is a great opportunity to expand your investment portfolio. If you've been wanting to acquire shares of Google or Amazon, generate cash using high-yield stocks or baby bonds (you'll learn about them in this book), or buy any of the other myriad investments that openly trade on the stock market, this is your opportunity to make those purchases.

Definitely discuss the potential use of this option with your financial advisor. The investments can easily be directly rolled out to your rollover IRA using the Trustee-to-Trustee Transfer method when you retire or sold at any time and the assets transferred back into your 401(k) if so desired.

Roth 401(k) Plans

Roth 401(k) plans work similarly to a Roth IRA (i.e., there are no current income tax savings), so a 15% savings of your gross income results in an actual 15% reduction to your net income. Investment options will be the same as in your company's traditional 401(k). But the gold key is, the savings and growth will eventually be withdrawn tax-free.

If you receive employer matching contributions to your 401(k) savings, note that the employer matching contributions *will go into your traditional 401(k) account.* There is no provision in the tax code around this, and the company contributions cannot be made into your Roth 401(k) account. The company contributions will be made to your traditional 401(k) account, which will be taxable on both contributions and earnings when later withdrawn.

With a Roth 401(k), there are a few special rules that you should know to avoid a tax "gotcha" moment.

Transferring an Existing Roth 401(k) to a New Employer's Roth 401(k)

If you leave one employer and get hired into another and, in the process, transfer your entire existing Roth 401(k) to your new employer's Roth 401(k), the number of years the account was open and existing in the original 401(k) plan will count for the five-year period required for qualified distributions. You must ensure that your previous employer provides your new employer with the appropriate account information detailing the date the original Roth 401(k) was opened and how much money had been contributed to it. However, if you only transfer a *partial* amount of your existing Roth 401(k) to the new employer's Roth 401(k), it will begin a new five-year qualifying period; you will lose whatever number of years it had originally.

This five-year clock is important to you. If you have five or more years to go before you retire, the best advice is to open a Roth 401(k) now, fund it with as much or as little as you want or can afford, and let the five-year clock begin.

Transferring an Existing Roth 401(k) to an Existing Roth IRA

If you transfer funds from your Roth 401(k) into your existing Roth IRA that you have had open for five or more years, the entire distribution to the Roth IRA will be a qualified distribution and meet the required minimum five-year rule. However, if your existing Roth IRA has existed for less than five years, the Roth 401(k) distribution to it will take on the same holding period as your existing Roth IRA.

Transferring an Existing Roth 401(k) to a New Roth IRA

If you transfer your existing Roth 401(k) to a new Roth IRA, the required five-year qualifying period will begin the year the new Roth IRA was opened, irrespective of how long your Roth 401(K) has been in existence.

The five-year clocks are important. If you have at least five years to go before you retire, the best advice is to open a Roth IRA and, as noted above, possibly a Roth 401(k) now, fund each with as much or as little as you want or can afford, and let the five-year clocks begin.

Google the item for the most current information and rules for each of the above savings plans.

Congress giveth and Congress taketh away.

Creating / Setting Up Your Contributions to Your Employer's 401(k) Plan

The first thing for you to do is to research the available investments in your company's 401(k) plan. Log on to their website and get an idea of the mutual funds that you are able to invest in. Compare them to the information in this book to get a general understanding of where they fall. Then click into each one to gain further information on the fund. Print that information if not too large or take notes.

With the information on the funds in hand, you can work with your financial advisor to determine which fund and what percentage you will invest into each. Or if going alone, use your age and health condition to help determine how risk intense or averse you should be with your selections. Here are some general guidelines, but you must be comfortable with your selections.

If in your 20s—5% MMF, 10% bonds, 85% stocks

30s—5% MMF, 15% bonds, 80% stocks
40s—10% MMF, 15% bonds, 75% stocks
50s—10% MMF, 25% bonds, 65% stocks
60s—15% MMF, 25% bonds, 60% stocks

Websites may differ slightly among the various companies sponsoring the plans, but the following should apply:

- Generally, you'll first need to enter the total percentage of your periodic paycheck that you wish to save; let's say 15% to begin with.
- Then advance to the screens with the list of investments that you may select from. Allocate the percent of each selection with the total of all the allocations equaling 100%. The 15% of your paycheck is equal to 100% of your investment allocation. Review and double-check the selections.
- Know which segment of the plan you are investing in, traditional 401(k) or Roth 401(k), and then submit.

Once you have made your selections and begun contributing, review your results at least once a year. Early January of each year would be a good time to do the review, so you'll have a full year of results to look over.

Business cycles will affect stock prices the most, so if stock values have come down, it may be a good time to redeploy some of the existing MMF and bond savings into additional stock purchases. If stocks have had a really good year and the percentage is skewed by more than 10%–15% from the targeted allocation, you may wish to reallocate by moving some of the stock profits over to the MMF and bond funds. Stay within a general percentage allocation for your existing savings as you redeploy your funds.

As you move up in age, reallocate your future savings per your advisory discussions or the general recommendations above. When ready to retire, work with your advisor to transfer your 401(k) savings to your IRA and reallocate for a comfortable, financially secure retirement at that time.

If you've been saving for thirty years or longer, your percentage-balanced 401(k) account should be showing some rather high numbers. Assuming you've reached or exceeded $1,000,000, you'll have amassed per the last allocation in the above example: $150,000 in MMF, $250,000 in bonds, and $600,000 in stocks. I think that's a pretty good send-off from your job and beats getting a gold watch. And if you've been socking it away in your IRA/Roth IRA as well, which I hope you have been doing, your retirement peace of mind, financially speaking, is even better than you ever first imagined.

To illustrate a sample of a 401(k) investment plan that uses a current allocation and then successive modifications over several years leading to retirement, please refer to Appendix A. There are also several online investment allocation calculators available, which you may wish to review. Just google "investment calculator" and take your pick from the list.

Need Cash? Better Think Twice before Taking a Loan from Your 401(k) Balance

While it may be possible, even easy, to take a loan from your 401(k) balance (up to 50% of the account, but no more than $50,000), it is not advisable to do so. You must repay the amount of the loan that was taken from your 401(k) account within a set period of time.

If you should fail to completely repay the loan within the time allotted—what happens if you suddenly lose your job?—the unpaid balance will be considered a distribution, and you will be tagged with a 10% penalty for the outstanding amount of the loan if under age 59½, plus the income tax. I have seen this happen on more than one occasion to people I knew and worked with.

Furthermore, your repayment to the plan is made entirely with after-tax dollars. *You do not get a tax break on the repayment amount.* In the end, you pay back the loan—*with interest*—with after-tax dollars that have now been taxed at your regular tax rate. Then when you eventually withdraw from your 401(k)—assuming during your retirement years—you will be taxed again at your regular tax rate on all the withdrawals. By taking a loan from your 401(k), you have walked into a double-tax situation on the same amount of money.

Seek other means to obtain your loans, but do not raid your 401(k) for an "easy" access loan. There is nothing easy to be said about being double-taxed.

When Relationships Fall Apart, Use a QDRO to Split Assets

Unfortunately, not all relationships last forever. If you find yourself in such a situation and your attorney doesn't discuss using a qualified domestic relations order (QDRO) to split your retirement assets with your spouse, you'll need to reference the attorney to it. The QDRO will transfer the retirement assets from one spouse to the other without setting off a taxable event. If you mistakenly withdraw half of your retirement assets to split and transfer to the other spouse yourself, you've just walked into a major tax "gotcha!" that you can't undo.

What Happens to Your IRA/401(k) When You've Reached Your Sell-By Date?

Assuming that your retirement plan beneficiary forms are current, the distribution and subsequent withdrawals will be made according to the beneficiary designations without going through probate. Distributions can be easy and simple to increasingly involved, depending on your beneficiary's relationship to you and whether you had begun distributions.

The simplest transfer is to a charity. There are no taxes to you or your estate for the transfer, and the charity receives the full amount of the account (or portion, if proportional).

The next easiest transfer is to a spouse, who has several options, including treating themselves as the owner if it is an IRA, or have the 401(k) plan administrator make a direct rollover to an IRA on their behalf. Nonspouse beneficiaries can never treat themselves as the owner, and there are other withdrawal rules for nonspouses to contend with.

Because of the increasing complexities going beyond leaving the account to a charity or your spouse, you should have your beneficiaries consult with a tax advisor on the distribution methods available to them *before* they take any amount from the account. With retirement plans, if you mess it up, the IRS is not forgiving, and a beneficiary could stand to lose a lot of money to unintended taxes.

With regard to your spouse or adult children as beneficiaries, if the account has tax obligations on withdrawals (i.e., non-Roth accounts), these beneficiaries may find themselves thrown into a higher tax bracket. Your spouse will now be filing their tax return at the single tax rate instead of the married filing joint tax rate, and their RMD could be significantly higher with the inclusion of your account.

With regard to your grown children, they could be in their prime earning years when they inherit your taxable retirement account. The required distributions for nonspousal inherited IRAs could result in moving your children significantly higher up in the tax bracket scales. Congress continues to discuss reducing the length of the withdrawal period to a maximum of only ten years. As of this publication, it is carried through the inheritor's lifetime (the stretch IRA). See https://www.foxbusiness.com/personal-finance/retirement-reform-stretch-ira-rule and https://www.investopedia.com/terms/s/stretch-ira.asp.

What you originally thought you were leaving to your beneficiaries may just be going to the government in the form of unintended taxes, as I'm sure you didn't plan to leave the government a windfall. This is another reason to consider Roth IRAs / Roth 401(k)s and conversions to Roth IRAs.

Final thoughts in this area: If you find you are unable or choose not to convert all your retirement savings to a Roth and are concerned about the potentially severe tax consequences to your beneficiaries, you may want to consider looking into purchasing a whole life insurance policy. A life insurance policy is received tax-free by the beneficiary.

This policy could help to cover the amount of inheritance that you intended for your beneficiaries to receive but now realize may be eaten up by taxes. To level the field, consider taking a negligible withdrawal from your retirement account—some small amount that you won't really miss during your lifetime—and purchasing a life insurance policy with it if you find yourself in this situation.

Another means to transfer your retirement assets to your intended beneficiaries would be to take larger withdrawals and make annual tax-free gifts to your intended recipients. For the 2019 tax year, you may gift up to $15,000 per person, tax-free. Your spouse may also make tax-free gifts of up to $15,000 per person; hence, each person could receive up to $30,000 in tax-free gifts each year.

Congress occasionally makes changes to the amount of the annual gift tax exclusion. To obtain the current tax-free annual gift limits, do an online search for "[year] gift tax exclusion."

Once gifted, the recipients can use the money any way they so choose. A helpful nudge in the right direction from you on how they may consider spending it wouldn't hurt (i.e., paying down their mortgage, seeking additional education, contributing to their retirement plans, etc.).

Blowing the gift on fun and games, beers and brats, or a rat-ted-out Porsche wouldn't be my idea of how to spend it, but once it's given, you have no say so on how it's spent. Of course, there's always the thought of dangling next year's gift over their heads. See https://www.irs.gov/businesses/small-businesses-self-employed/ frequently-asked-questions-on-gift-taxes.

Retirement And Your 401(K) Plans

Upon retirement from your current employer and if you are at least 55 years of age, you may begin drawing from your traditional 401(k) without any penalty. Unless an exception applies, as earlier discussed with company stock that may be taxed at capital gains tax rates, you will still incur taxes at your ordinary income tax rates on the amounts that you do withdraw. Roth 401(k)s continue to fall under the rules for qualification (age 59½ and held for five years) and will be taxed and penalized on the earnings portion if withdrawn prior to full qualification.

If you can hold off withdrawing from your 401(k) for a few more years, until you are at least 59½, then it would be advisable to roll out your 401(k) investments to your IRA using the Trustee-to-Trustee Transfer method discussed in this chapter. Also note that most plans will require smaller account balances, $5,000 or less, to be either cashed out or rolled out. The reasons you want to roll out your 401(k) and not cash out your 401(k) will become very clear in the next paragraphs.

Plan administrators are required to withhold 20% from each 401(k) distribution for federal income tax and an appropriate amount for state income tax if that applies to your situation. Your 1099-R statement at the end of the year will show the *entire amount, including the amount that was withheld for taxes*, as a taxable income withdrawal. Not fair, I agree, but that's how it works.

What this means in dollars is that if you want to receive $50,000 in your hand, you'll need to withdraw $62,500 at the minimum (and that's just to cover the *federal* tax withholding obligation). In this example, it represents at least $12,500 of your retirement savings that is no longer invested and working for you.

Sure, you may get some of the tax withholding back when you file your tax return the following year, but you're still out that amount in your tax-deferred account. Kind of defeats the purpose, eh?

This 20% federal withholding rate applies to you even if you are in the lowest of tax brackets when making the withdrawal directly from your 401(k). You have no say so in the matter.

Further adding insult to injury, because of the larger amount of money that must be withdrawn to meet your in-hand cash needs, the withdrawal may move you into an unexpectedly higher tax bracket. If you were considering taking a withdrawal from your 401(k), it is probably time for you to rethink this plan of action. Make the better decision to roll out your savings to your IRA, where you can withdraw and be taxed only on the amount of money you actually need.

Do yourself a favor and don't fall into this money-gobbling tax trap if you can avoid it. Roll out your 401(k) investments to an IRA and hold off until you are at least 59½ before withdrawing.

Are You Still Working Past Age 72?

If you are still working past age 72, you may continue to contribute to your 401(k), and you are not required to begin RMDs of your 401(k) with your current employer *until* you are retired. However, any 401(k)s that may have been left with former employers *must have their RMDs begun at age 72.*

401(k) Plans Require a Separate RMD Calculation

RMDs for 401(k)s are calculated separately from RMDs for IRAs. If you are in the RMD age zone and have both a traditional IRA and a 401(k), *you must calculate and* separately *withdraw an*

RMD from each account. Failure to properly withdraw the full amount from either type of account gets you into the *50% penalty* box on the amount of money that was required to be withdrawn but wasn't. If your 401(k) RMD requires you to withdraw $20,000 and you only withdraw $5,000, your penalty is $7,500!

Use Only the Trustee-to-Trustee Transfer When Moving from a 401(k) to an IRA

When moving to another employer or retiring, you will probably want to transfer your 401(k) to an IRA. When transferring investments from a 401(k) to an IRA (either a rollover IRA—see below—or an existing traditional IRA), you should only use the Trustee-to-Trustee Transfer method, (i.e., have the 401(k) administrator transfer your investments directly to your IRA trustee). Do not have the assets sent to you, or you will likely end up in a potentially short-window time trap that may trigger unwanted tax consequences and potential penalties. Always use a Trustee-to-Trustee Transfer to move your assets from one place to the other and eliminate the headaches.

Provide your IRA trustee with copies of your most recent 401(k) statements, showing your investments, amounts, and other pertinent information. The IRA trustee will open the IRA if it is a new IRA and provide you with the account number. They will then coordinate with the 401(k) trustee for the transfer of the investments. All in all, this behind-the-scenes process could take two or more weeks to complete.

Transfer Your 401(k) Investments "In Kind" or Convert Them to Cash

If you do not specify in writing to the IRA and 401(k) administrators to move your 401(k) investments to your IRA *in kind*, thus retaining the same investments you have, the 401(k) administrator will sell the investments in your 401(k) and transfer the cash proceeds to your IRA. This is the default if not specified otherwise, and the 401(k) administrator will usually not inquire if you want your investments transferred *in kind.* If you don't speak up, the 401(k) administrator will by default sell those investments and transfer the cash.

If you are happy with the investments in your 401(k), you probably do not want the administrator to sell them. This bears repeating. If you do not specify to the 401(k) administrator to transfer your investments *in kind,* the administrator will automatically sell them. *You must be proactive and specify in writing to move the assets in kind,* thereby ensuring your assets move as you want them to, and not as cash.

One problem that may occur with requesting an *in kind* transfer is if the receiving IRA institution isn't able to accept the particular 401(k) investment as *in kind.* Certain 401(k) investments may be specifically created for an employer's organization (institutional class) and are not available outside of that 401(k) plan. In such cases, the investment will have to be sold and the cash proceeds transferred. However, there may be similar "investor class" investments of the same type available in your IRA as were in your 401(k). The IRA administrator should help you identify these similar investments in their IRA offerings.

Annuities

Annuities are insurance company products designed to provide recurring income generally paid to you on a monthly basis. Immediate annuities begin payments to you the very next month and every month thereafter. Anything other than an immediate annuity is a gimmick.

If you select a lifetime payment plan and you expire before receiving all your initial investment, the annuity may be structured to pay any unused, unpaid remaining investment amount to your heir. However, if you select a *term certain* annuity, it will pay you for your lifetime, for at least a specific minimum number of years. Once that certain period has passed and you expire, nothing will be passed to your heir.

As you approach retirement age, you may begin receiving free "dinner" invitations where financial advice will be presented to you. The presenter will typically show you a number of charts and numbers and end the presentation by setting up an appointment with you (and your spouse if married) where you will be encouraged to invest in one of the annuities of the day. Selling just one $100,000 indexed annuity will generate more than enough commission for the salesperson to pay for the meals of the entire room of attendees.

If you want to go out for the meal and listen to the presentation, that is fine. You may be able to pick up on information that you weren't aware of before attending. But don't become the fish on the hook.

My recommendation is to stay away from deferred annuities, variable annuities, indexed annuities, and anything that is *not* an immediate annuity. The fees associated with annuity products, other than an immediate annuity, are, in my opinion, not worth the price of admission. You should be able to do much better investing elsewhere with lower fees and then use that value to purchase an immediate annuity if you so choose. Anything other than an immediate annuity pays the highest commissions to the salespeople selling them. *Guess which annuity they want to sell to you?* You should *buy* the annuity that you need and not the first annuity that the salesperson wants to offer to *sell* to you.

Because immediate annuities are issued subject to the prevailing interest rates at the time and a person's or couple's age, if you decide to purchase them, *laddering* your purchase of immediate annuities may be the better idea. Investing $50,000–$100,000 in an immediate annuity, followed a year or so later by another immediate annuity, and still another immediate annuity later on may be something to consider. Although interest rates may change in the interim (up or down), you will also be aging in the process, which may offset any interest rate decline while providing a larger total monthly income stream; and if it is a lifetime benefit, you will never run out of money.

Be absolutely sure that you understand everything about the annuity that you are considering buying. Once the money is turned over and the annuity has started, you are locked in.

If you purchase your immediate annuity inside of a Roth IRA, the Roth tax rules apply, and the periodic payments to you will be received tax-free as long as you have passed the Roth qualification requirements. If you purchase your immediate annuity in a traditional or rollover IRA, each periodic payment to you will be fully taxable as received. Annuities purchased in these types of IRAs are not included in the amounts used for figuring the annual RMD (i.e., they're already in process of being "distributed" to you).

If you purchase your annuity in a taxable account (using money you've already paid taxes on), a portion of each payment received will be tax-free as a return of your investment. The balance will be taxable.

Speaking from personal experience, here is something else to think about with anything other than an immediate annuity. If you are absolutely convinced to invest in something other than an immediate annuity, don't permit the salesperson to place the annuity into your IRA (I didn't know better at the time, and I trusted the smooth-talking salesperson). A deferred annuity (if it's not immediate, it's deferred) already qualifies for income tax deferral until you begin taking payments.

I have read recently where the school of thought on this point has been shifting (i.e., it is okay to put a deferred annuity into your IRA). I don't agree with this and recommend that you do not squander your ability to save and invest in your tax-deferred IRA by substituting an already tax-deferred annuity in its place.

Look at deferred annuities last and only after you've maxed out your IRAs and 401(k)s and are looking for additional tax-deferred investments.

Mutual Funds

Unless you are invested directly in individual stocks or bonds, the majority of your preretirement investments will likely be invested in mutual funds in your employer's 401(k) plan. Mutual funds will also likely be the predominant investment held in your IRA/Roth IRA, so a discussion of funds and their costs is definitely relative to your understanding and investment decision-making process.

Closed-end funds are issued with a set number of shares by the investment company and trade similarly to stocks. Closed-end funds are not discussed in this book, and if interested, you should thoroughly research them on your own.

This discussion concerns only open-ended mutual funds, which are the type of investment product typically offered in an employer's 401(k) plan and purchased in an IRA. Open-ended mutual funds continually issue new shares as investment contributions are received by the investment company.

In IRAs, such funds may occasionally close to new investors for a period of time or permanently. This usually occurs because the fund or the fund's manager has received rave reviews for outstanding performance, and the money comes pouring in faster than it can be invested by the manager. In such instances, they need to take a time out and will reopen the fund to new investors at a later time.

Fidelity Magellan is one mutual fund that comes to mind. As a managed fund, it had outperformed for several years and drew intense investor interest. As a result, it was forced to close to new investors as management struggled to find investment opportunities in the market for the cash that poured in. Current investors could still contribute, but no new investors were permitted to purchase shares.

Dodge & Cox Stock, another long-standing premier managed stock fund, closes and reopens periodically to new investors. It has done this for as long as I can remember following the market.

Generally, a person may purchase mutual funds in their investment company account that have been issued by other nonaffiliated investment companies, Fidelity Investment products purchased in a Schwab account, Vanguard investment products purchased in a TD Ameritrade account, etc. However, certain popular funds may only be available to investors directly through the issuing investment company and not obtainable through other investment organizations. Vanguard Wellington, a very old and respected balanced fund, has only been available to investors who are Vanguard investment account holders (or in 401(k) plans where Vanguard provides the plan management).

If you are looking to purchase a mutual fund in your IRA or taxable account and find it is either closed or otherwise unobtainable, one of the above reasons is probably the cause. A little research may indicate when a "closed to new investors" fund will reopen to the public.

What Are Mutual Funds?

So what are mutual funds? Mutual funds are a package of securities composed of pooled investor assets—yours and thousands of others—with an *investment company*, which then purchases various stocks, bonds, and money markets. The assembled assets are then packaged for sale by the investment company as "funds" with the name closely resembling its array of assets. Information regarding its underlying investment composition, management's flexibility with investment purchases, historical performance, and management fees are provided to potential investors in what is called a prospectus.

Each time an investor opens a new fund, they must be provided a prospectus detailing that pertinent information. However, oftentimes the prospectus may be a year old or older, and things may have changed in the interim. You should read this document and question anything that troubles you. See https://investor.vanguard.com/mutual-funds/list#/mutual-funds/asset-class/month-end-returns.

Fund Fees

Mutual funds may be sold with or without an additional sales fee (load funds or no-load funds). Load funds may be front-end or back-end loaded. A front-end loaded fund means that for every dollar you invest, only 95¢, or less, will be invested and put to work for you. The other nickel goes to the salesperson's commission.

Back-end loaded funds, also known as a contingent deferred sales charge, means the salesperson's commission is paid to them up front by the investment company, so each full dollar of your investment immediately goes to work for you. However, if you decide to sell and exit the investment, you will be tagged with a declining percentage fee over a period of up to ten years. This is to compensate the investment company for the commission it paid to the salesperson when you initially purchased the fund. *Pay me now or pay me later.*

You can avoid the sales *load* entirely by purchasing only *no-load* funds, which are mutual funds that are sold without the front- or back-end sales charge. Most Schwab, Fidelity, T. Rowe Price, TD Ameritrade, and Vanguard *company* products are no load. These are mutual funds created, packaged, and managed by the investment company.

However, if you are using the services of an advisor, you should expect to pay a separate advisory fee of one sort or the other. If you are utilizing no-load funds in your account, the advisory service may have a fee applicable to the amount of assets under management. This was explained earlier with the fee comparison chart and recommendation to use front-end loaded funds as a lower long-term advisory cost. If making your own planning and investing decisions, you won't incur the additional advisory costs.

All mutual funds, regardless of their structure (i.e., front-end/back-end contingent load or no load), have ongoing management fees that are built into the operation of the fund and included in the results of the fund's annual published performance. Someone needs to be paid to construct and monitor the assets in the fund, and you can't get around them.

These management fees are in addition to and separate from any advisory service fees you may pay for help with your investments. Even DIYers pay the fund management fees—they are baked into the fund.

Some funds may also have advertising fees (referred to as 12b-1 fees) in addition to their management fees. This is to pay for the fluff and fancy brochures. You don't need that stuff, and you'll want to avoid those funds charging that extra fee.

Why Are Mutual Fund Fees Important to You?

Fees reduce the annual returns of the fund and over time can add up to a significantly large amount of money. That is why as an investor, you must review the prospectus to determine the ongoing management fees that will affect the total returns to you. The larger your investment in a high-fee fund grows, the greater the amount of money those fees will be extracted from your growth.

This is just one more reason to consider why passively managed index funds frequently outperform actively managed funds.

According to NerdWallet.com, an initial $25,000 investment in a US mid-cap blended fund earning a 7% annual return with a 1.02% ongoing management expense ratio and adding another $10,000 to the account each year over a forty-year investment span will lose approximately 25% in value to the ongoing management fees. The larger the portfolio, the more an investor will pay in fees over time. See the following (https://www.nerdwallet.com/blog/investing/millennial-retirement-fees-one-percent-half-million-savings-impact/):

Number of Years Invested	Portfolio Value Lost to Fees	After-Fee Investment Value	Value Lost to Fees
10	$11,343	$166,000	6.4%
20	$61,696	$435,001	12.4%
30	$210,700	$914,215	18.7%
40	$592,798	$1,770,000	25.1%

This is further illustrated in a graph at the Securities and Exchange Commission (SEC) website. See https://www.sec.gov/investor/alerts/ib_fees_expenses.pdf.

Portfolio Value from Investing $100,000 over
Twenty Years, with a 4% Annual Return

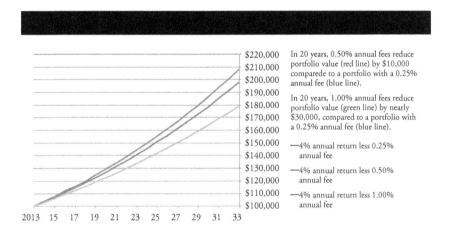

$220,000
$210,000 In 20 years, 0.50% annual fees reduce portfolio value (red line) by $10,000 comparede to a portfolio with a 0.25% annual fee (blue line).
$200,000
$190,000 In 20 years, 1.00% annual fees reduce portfolio value (green line) by nearly $30,000, compared to a portfolio with a 0.25% annual fee (blue line).
$180,000
$170,000
$160,000
$150,000 —4% annual return less 0.25% annual fee
$140,000
$130,000 —4% annual return less 0.50% annual fee
$120,000
$110,000 —4% annual return less 1.00% annual fee
$100,000

2013 15 17 19 21 23 25 27 29 31 33

Another general example of the impact of fees on an investment's growth can be found at the Vanguard website. See https://investor.vanguard.com/investing/how-to-invest/impact-of-costs.

How Are Mutual Funds Priced?

Mutual funds are priced per share at the end of each trading day (which is their NAV [net asset value]) and are purchased (or sold) per a specified amount of money at that time. Unlike stocks, mutual funds do not trade throughout the day; they trade only at the end of the day. I've known of funds where the minimum to invest was $25,000. Most funds that are generally available to the public will let you initially invest for between $2,000 and $3,000 and oftentimes less for IRA purchases, for which you will receive whole and partial shares for the amount invested.

With no-load funds, other than the ongoing built-in management fee, there are generally no additional fees imposed for purchasing or selling shares. Investment companies will usually restrict your buying and selling of the same fund within a short period of time. If you sell, you will usually be barred from repurchasing the same fund for up to ninety days. This is to protect other investors from those who are attempting to do market timing. Selling shares in the fund reduces the amount of money in it, which affects the NAV, which affects other investors. You'll more than likely encounter this in your company's 401(k) plan investment offerings. If you are interested in day trading, use ETFs (described further below) or individual stocks in your IRA/Roth IRA, but don't try to day-trade mutual funds.

I have found that the only important time to be interested in the market, as concerns mutual funds, is the last ten to fifteen minutes of the trading day. If the market in general is up at that time, NAV will likely be higher at the end of the day when the trades in mutual funds occur, so this is a good time to sell your shares, if selling. However, if the market in general is lower at this point, then this is the time to submit your purchase order, if buying. *Buy low, sell high.* The other six hours and fifteen minutes of the trading day doesn't really mean much as far as the effect on the NAV of mutual funds go. Go for a walk or play with the dog.

Stock Mutual Funds

Stock mutual funds consist predominantly of the stocks of publicly traded companies and are typically held for capital gain purposes. Stock funds are available in indexed, specialized, balanced, growth, value, retirement target date-specific, international (only non-US companies), global (foreign and US companies), broadly based or limited in scope, REITs (real estate investment trusts) and so on, as there are literally thousands of funds available. See https:// www.statista.com/topics/1441/mutual-funds/.

Actively managed funds have higher fees than do index funds (which track a particular segment of the market). However, just because a fund has active management doesn't guarantee that it will equal or outperform a given index. While theoretically possible, it is most difficult to beat the index consistently over time.

Actively managed funds will typically, but not always, have a high portfolio turnover and are not advisable for taxable accounts (called the *turnover ratio* and found within the fund's prospectus). This is due to the higher annual tax consequences that are generated by churning (*lots of trading*) the underlying holdings in the fund. I recommend that you hold high turnover funds only in tax-deferred or tax-free accounts; otherwise, expect to receive a tax bill at the end of the year.

Stock funds that swing annual returns wildly one way or the other are considered aggressive and have a large standard deviation. *Tread carefully here.* Better to invest in more even-tempered funds with mild to moderate deviation producing fairly consistent annual returns. Look for funds with base hits rather than those that swing for home runs. The latter often strike out.

Recall the story of the tortoise and the hare. Take it slow, and you'll eventually arrive. And think about this for a minute: Mathematically, it takes a 25% increase to get back to even after suffering a 20% loss. A 50% loss requires a 100% gain! How long will it take your investment to regain 25% or 100%? Suffering a large paper loss will probably have you thinking about selling; if you do sell, it guarantees you will lock in your loss.

Stock funds will distribute capital gains periodically, but more importantly, usually during December, as fund managers adjust their portfolio holdings to improve their annual outlook to investors. If the fund is held in a tax-deferred or tax-free account, this distribution and shuffling of investments in the fund doesn't matter to you as regards any current tax year issues.

However, if shares of the fund are purchased in a taxable account in early December and the fund makes a distribution, the value of each share will *decrease* by a certain amount and the number of shares you own in the fund will *increase* by a certain amount. The net–net effect will be a $0 gain or loss to you; you will now own more shares, but of a lesser value per share. You will have accidentally stumbled into a taxable event, even if you only held the shares for one day, and you will receive a 1099 at the end of the year requiring you to owe taxes (although you have not profited even 1¢). Consider investing earlier in the year and participate in this year-end tax problem as a winner.

Bond Mutual Funds

Similar to their stock mutual fund cousins, bond mutual funds invest in a variety of publicly traded bonds. Indexed, specialized, taxable, tax-free (municipals), corporate, the list goes on and on. Bond funds of all sorts are typically held for income purposes, diversification, and tax relief.

Unlike individual bonds, bond funds do not have specified maturity dates. Investment company desk traders in bonds are constantly buying and selling the bonds in the fund, typically not holding any bonds to their maturity, so by default, the funds themselves do not have a specified maturity date. Because of this, there is the potential that an investor in bond funds can lose money whereas investors in individual bonds are guaranteed by the issuer to receive the face value of the bond upon its maturity (or some recourse).

The per share price and underlying value of bond funds will change depending on the prevailing Fed Funds Rate. As Fed rates rise, the value of existing bonds will fall. As Fed rates fall, the value of existing bonds will rise.

Example:

Extend your arms like the wings of a plane and then tilt your "wings." Get the idea?

Newly issued bonds will generally pay an amount equal to or just over the Fed rate based on the perceived riskiness of the bond. When the Fed adjusts their rates, short-term bond fund prices will move the least. Long-term bond funds will change share pricing the most. A 1% change in the Fed rate will move the value of long-term bond funds a minimum of 10%. Consider staying with short-term or intermediate-term bond funds for more worry-free nights.

Tax-free municipal bonds should best be held in taxable accounts, not IRAs, and are better suited for those in a higher tax bracket. The higher the person's regular tax bracket, the better tax-free municipal bonds will serve their income requirements.

Money Market Funds

Money market funds (MMF), also known as stable value funds, invest in various high credit rating short-term debt obligations in both taxable and tax-free portfolios. Businesses will issue short-term paper/notes of 90- to 180-day duration and up to a full year to raise working capital for their operations.

Mutual fund organizations that invest in these debt obligations are paid by the businesses and will pass the interest received, minus their fees, on to the MMF investor. It's important to note that MMFs are not government guaranteed as are bank money market *accounts*. The two should not be confused with each other.

MMFs tend to maintain the sacred value of $1 per share and will adjust or often eliminate their management fees to compensate for the general market situation at that time. For this reason, MMFs are considered very safe and pose a low risk to the investor. However, in a very limited number of cases since MMFs were first introduced in 1971, only a few firms have "broken the dollar" and returned less than $1 per share to the investor. See https://www.investopedia.com/articles/mutualfund/08/money-market-break-buck.asp.

Therefore, you must review the fund's prospectus to determine its underlying investments and management's prerogative for their potential to be problematic in this regard. If the MMF is permitted to invest in any wild, speculative opportunity that management desires, it is probably not where you want to put your money. I have found that the money market funds available through the company-sponsored 401(k) plans where I had my savings and my IRA where I currently have my savings have generally passed the test for assuring the continued stability of $1 per share.

Mutual fund MMFs will typically pay close to the average one-year CD rate of return, which is higher than traditional bank savings account or bank money market account interest rates. MMFs are generally available for withdrawal at any time by the customer (versus a CD's early withdrawal penalties). However, the investor needs to understand that MMFs are not guaranteed by the US government.

What Are Money Market Funds Typically Used For?

MMFs are typically where you store your investment dollars after selling an investment or accumulate your cash resources when riding out a business cycle while waiting to make an opportune investment. If you are looking for longer-term US government-guaranteed safe savings with potentially higher returns, look into *laddering* five-year CDs or short-term US Treasury issues. SWAN.

Individual Stocks, Bonds, And Other Investments

Individual Stocks

Newly issued shares from a company, typically offered via an IPO (initial program offering), forms the primary market. However, most shares are traded in the secondary market. Unless you're participating in an IPO, when you purchase stock shares, you are doing so with shares that were issued earlier and bought by someone else. In other words, you are trading in what is called the secondary market or, more commonly called, the stock market.

You can generally avoid the annual capital gain/loss tax issues found with a taxable account until such time of your choosing by owning and holding individual stocks and only selling them when it fits your needs. The value of stocks can rise/fall without consequence to your tax situation until such time as you decide to sell. At that time, you will recognize a capital gain or loss on the sale.

Stocks are priced per share and are purchased or sold by the number of whole shares. Sales fees for purchasing or selling are typically one set price no matter how many shares you purchase or sell. Stocks will trade all day long while the markets are open, and prices can fluctuate wildly throughout the trading day. Shares are held electronically in your account, unless you request actual physical paper shares (not recommended).

Stocks that generate periodic dividends (typically each quarter) will create short-term taxable events with each dividend if not held in a tax-deferred/tax-free account. Investments in American companies generally throw off "qualified" dividends, which receive preferential tax treatment. Dividends can either be reinvested (at no cost) to purchase more of the same company shares or can be directed to your settlement fund, typically your money market fund.

Stocks that pay high dividends are also referred to as pseudo-bonds and are held mainly for the income generated each quarter. Their share price fluctuation is often of secondary concern to their investors.

When a company generates a dividend, it announces the dividend in advance and provides several important dates with which you should be familiar. The *declaration date* is when the board of directors announces the forthcoming dividend. The *settlement date* is when the date of ownership must be recorded. The *ex-dividend date* is when the shares trade with the value of the dividend initially discounted from the share price. And the *paid date* is when the dividend is paid out.

To be entitled to receive the dividend, you must be listed as the registered owner. Since it takes two (2) days from your purchase of a stock to be listed in the [electronic] books as the owner, you must purchase the shares three days ahead of the *settlement date* to be sure you're listed as the registered owner. If you purchase the shares within less than three days of the *settlement date,* the dividends will go to the previous owner of the shares.

Stocks generally will initially trade at a slightly reduced price on the *ex-dividend date*, as the value of the shares will be discounted due to the dividend payout. The *paid date* is the date when you can expect the dividend to be applied to your account, either purchasing additional shares if reinvested or deposited as cash to your settlement account.

Investing guru Warren Buffett said, and I paraphrase, "Don't invest in anything that you're not willing to hold on to for at least ten years." This enables you to ride the business cycle of ups and downs in the price of the shares.

Educated investing is fine, such as share prices increasing around tax filing time as investors seek to fund their IRAs, but don't try to time the market. It's not market timing that counts but time *in* the market. If you get psyched out and sell when a stock stumbles, you set yourself up for a real loss. The idea is to buy low and sell high (or never sell and pass the shares to your beneficiary, a very nice way, taxwise, to receive taxable investments).

Another saying from an unknown author goes like this, "Only invest in stocks that go up. If the stock doesn't go up, don't invest in it." This last comment is a joke, in case you missed that.

Rule of thumb: Invest $1 today and expect it to be worth 89¢ tomorrow. Live with it. It happens, and it took me awhile to console myself with it. If losing 11¢ (or 20¢ or 30¢) makes you gasp for air and rush to sell the investment, stay out of the market because you'll only lose your money. Take it in stride and look long-term.

Shares of company stock are issued as either *common* or *preferred*. In addition to issuing common shares as the majority of company stock, the banking/finance industry segment is big into issuing preferred shares, which may pay a higher dividend than their common shares.

Preferred shares of stock guarantee the payment of dividends *before* shareholders of common stock can receive even 1¢ of dividends and generally pay a higher yield than common stock. In the distribution scheme of things, bond holders take precedence over preferred shareholders, then preferred over common, then common. Most shares you purchase will be of the common stock variety.

I recommend against you investing in individual stocks unless your portfolio is valued over $300,000. If it is, then you may begin to explore beyond mutual funds, but be very careful. Who would have thought that GM, GE, Kodak, and many other big-name companies could have the market problems they've had?

As a general rule, do not invest more than you could afford to lose in any one stock and no more than $50,000 invested in any one stock. Otherwise, just stick with mutual funds (or their ETF cousins, explained below).

Famed investment advisor Richard Rainwater once said on the PBS TV show *Wall Street Week* with Louis Rukeyser, "If you want to get rich, concentrate. If you want to stay rich, diversify." Diversify for sure, but be very, very careful with concentrating your investments. The bottom can fall out in the blink of an eye.

ADR (American Depositary Receipt)

ADRs represent securities of foreign stock that trade on the US stock exchanges.

> An American depositary receipt (ADR) is a negotiable certificate issued by a U.S. depository bank representing a specified number of shares—or as little as one share—investment in a foreign company's stock. The ADR trades on markets in the U.S. as any stock would trade.
>
> ADRs represent a feasible, liquid way for U.S. investors to purchase stock in companies abroad. Foreign firms also benefit from ADRs, as they make it easier to attract American investors and capital—without the hassle and expense of listing themselves on U.S. stock exchanges. The certificates also provide access to foreign listed companies that would not be open to U.S. investment otherwise. (Investopedia)

Individual Bonds

US government bonds are not discussed here.

Bonds are corporate or municipal debt. These can be corporate bonds of various investment grades or "junk" ratings or municipal (muni) bonds of comparable ratings, which are generally considered tax-free unless... You'll need to dig into the nitty-gritty as not all muni bonds are completely tax-free, depending on what civic project the municipal bond money was raised to support.

Bonds of all sorts are typically held by investors for recurring income purposes. Stocks are held for the anticipation of capital appreciation.

Individual bonds are a bit more difficult for the individual investor to select and invest in due to the generally higher cost per bond ($1,000–$10,000), and which bonds should you buy? It may be better to invest in bond mutual funds and leave the selection to the pros.

Bond owners generally have protection under bankruptcy laws and as debt holders give them first rights to compensation. Generally speaking, that is. However, in the case of GM bondholders not all that long ago, historically accepted bankruptcy protection provisions were ignored and overruled by the US government. So be careful if thinking about holding individual bonds.

Bond prices will fluctuate based on Fed interest rates. However, if held to maturity, individual bonds will pay the face amount to the holder. This does not occur with bond mutual funds, which, by their nature, never mature.

If purchased at less than the face value of the bond, it is a *discounted* bond. If purchased at more than face value, you are paying a *premium* for the bond.

At maturity, you will only receive the face value of the bond (although you'll receive a given *yield* a few times *per* year, calculated on the bond's coupon and what you initially paid for the bond itself). If the yield is the *same* as the bond's coupon at purchase, then it is trading at *par*. If the yield is *higher* than the stated coupon, the bond is trading at a discount. And if the yield is *less* than the stated coupon, the bond is trading at a premium.

Some bonds as issued can be *called* before their scheduled maturity date. Calling a bond accelerates its maturity date. This typically occurs when a bond is issued with a coupon payment that is higher than others of same or similar investment grade status. You'll want to check if the bond is callable or not before you make your purchase decision.

If the bond issuer believes their financial ratings will improve such that they could issue new bonds with a lower coupon at some point in the future, thereby saving their company money, they will issue their bonds with the call feature and, if things improve financially, call the bond. A bond is typically not called within less than five years from its date of issuance. The purchaser can view such a bond as a pseudo five-year "not US government guaranteed" CD, confident that they will receive the periodic yield payment for at least five years, if not longer.

If the bond is called, the purchaser will receive the face value of the bond (along with the interest payments received in the interim). So buy your bonds either at par or at discount, but not at a premium, unless really needing the periodic income generated by such a bond.

Baby Bonds

A recent development in the bond arena is something called a baby bond or a snippet. Companies purchase full bonds from issuers and subdivide them into more affordable pieces, typically priced at $25 per share on introduction.

The baby bond / snippet will fluctuate in value per the Fed Funds Rate; however, they are issued with a stated coupon and may be callable in five years from issuance. To ensure you receive the full coupon (or more), purchase these at or below $25 per share.

Purchasing below $25 per share, your yield will be greater than the stated coupon. Purchasing above $25 per share, your yield will be less than the stated coupon. The interest paid on these baby bonds comes in like clockwork.

With a minimum five-year window before most newly issued baby bonds can be called, I personally use them for my own investing as five-year CD *substitutes*, paying better than five-year CD rates of interest, albeit without any US government guarantees.

Google "baby bonds" to see what it's all about. And see https://www.barrons.com/articles/at-ts-baby-bonds-offer-6-plus-yields-51545298200.

Zero-Coupon Bonds

A zero-coupon bond is a debt security that doesn't pay interest (a coupon) but is traded at a deep discount, rendering profit at maturity when the bond is redeemed for its full face value. Some zero-coupon bonds are issued as such, while others are bonds that have been stripped of their coupons by a financial institution and then repackaged as zero-coupon bonds. Because they offer the entire payment at maturity, zero-coupon bonds tend to fluctuate in price much more than coupon bonds. (Investopedia, https://www.investopedia.com/terms/z/zero-couponbond.asp)

Also see the Security and Exchange Commission's Investor.gov website: https://www.investor.gov/additional-resources/general-resources/glossary/zero-coupon-bond.

I have seen *zeros* trade for huge cap gains when interest rates were high and falling. Back when I was an MBA student and interest rates were falling, I was surprised to see such strong performance. Interest on zeros are not paid until the bond matures, but for tax purposes, interest is imputed annually. Because of this tax implication, hold zeros only in tax-deferred or tax-free accounts or hold a tax-exempt zero inside a taxable account. Zeros may be considered for relatively safe *long-term* planning needs (i.e., children's college tuition).

ETFs (Exchange-Traded Funds)

ETFs are a mixed security, a cross between a mutual fund and a stock. These are products assembled by financial organizations pooling investments similar to mutual funds, but unlike mutual funds, they trade on the stock exchange throughout the day as do stocks. ETFs may have lower management fees than similarly invested mutual funds. Some ETFs are sold without a sales fee; others are sold with a fee that is similar to the charges imposed when purchasing shares of individual stock.

ETFs are available that closely mimic similarly invested mutual funds, and investors have flocked to ETFs for their ability to trade at any time during the day. In general, ETFs tend to have lower management fees and lower buy-in price points (recall the minimum buy-ins of mutual funds) and can be potentially tax efficient compared to similar mutual funds.

MLP (Master Limited Partnerships)

> A master limited partnership (MLP) is a business venture that exists in the form of a publicly traded limited partnership. It combines the tax benefits of a private partnership—profits are taxed only when investors receive distributions—with the liquidity of a publicly-traded company.
>
> Like stocks, MLPs trade on national exchanges. MLPs are situated to take advantage of cash flow, as they are required to distribute all available cash to investors. MLPs can help reduce the cost of capital in capital-intensive businesses, such as the energy sector.
>
> The first MLP was organized in 1981. However, by 1987, Congress effectively limited the use of them to the real estate and natural resources sectors. These limitations were put into place out of a concern over too much lost corporate tax revenue since MLPs do not pay federal income taxes. (Investopedia)

My recommendation is that you do not invest in master limited partnerships inside an IRA unless you are looking to generate income for your tax preparer. MLPs generate K-1 tax forms, not 1099s. K-1s are generally more difficult to work with inside the confines of an IRA, but not overly complicated to work with in a taxable account. MLPs are perfectly acceptable to hold in a taxable account and generate some of the highest recurring incomes.

Stock Options

Stock options are a way to gamble in the market, as if the market itself weren't a gamble. Stock options traders use what are known as *puts* and *calls*.

An investor may purchase a *put* option if they expect a particular stock to fall. If the price of the stock falls, you put it to the other investor—the other investor must purchase the shares at the price of the put—and make them pay the higher price for the shares per the put.

An investor may purchase a *call* option if they expect the stock to rise. If the price of the stock rises, you call the shares away from the other investor at the lower price per the call, and they must sell the shares to you at that lower price.

Of course, the investors on the other end of the put and call options are betting the opposite of the issue and are selling the put/call options in the hope of profiting from the transaction and not having to take any action with regard to their shares. Unless you know exactly what you are doing and can afford to pay the costs associated with engaging in stock options trading, I recommend that you don't do it.

DIY—How To Purchase Investments Online

If you are a do-it-yourself investor, purchasing your investments online as an individual and not through or with the assistance of a broker, you will need to keep several things in mind to avoid potential problems with the trade:

1. You will need to have sufficient funds in your money market fund / settlement account to cover the costs of the purchase (*trade*) and sales fee (usually around $8 per trade, each way).

2. Always use a *limit* order for your trade and not a *market* order. With a limit order, you specify your purchase (or selling) price of the security. If the security hits your order's limit price, it will execute. If it does not hit the limit price, see the comments in no. 5 below.
    A market order means to execute the trade (buying or selling) right now, no matter what the price happens to be.
    If you are making a purchase in your IRA/Roth IRA, you'll definitely need to specify a limit on your purchase price, or the security could take an unexpected jump in price. And if buying *at market*, go well beyond the money that you have available for trading in your account.

3. You'll need to specify the *number of shares* if buying a stock, an ETF, or a bond. If buying a mutual fund, simply specify the amount of money you wish to invest in the fund.

4. You'll need to *identify the investment* you are purchasing or selling by using its trading symbol. For example, MSFT is Microsoft's symbol, T identifies AT&T, VZ is Verizon's, AAPL is Apple's symbol, and VWELX is Vanguard Wellington's mutual fund symbol. Note: All mutual fund symbols end in X. Money market mutual fund symbols end in XX.

5. You will need to state if your order is good for *today only* or if it is good *until cancelled*. If good for today only and the security does not execute at your specified limit price, the order will expire at the end of the day.

   If specified as good until cancelled, this will usually be held in the order queue for up to sixty days. If by the end of the sixtieth day the security has not traded at your specified limit price, the order will expire and close out. Companies will generally cap your limit order to around 5% or so, plus/minus of the current trading price when you place your order. They don't want your order clogging their system forever if you were to put in an order to buy that is unrealistically far and away from the current trading price of the security.

6. You will need to specify if you are buying or selling. *Buy. Sell. Buy. Sell.* Click the *appropriate* button. Doubly notated per comments I received, as one of my reviewers noted that he had mistakenly selected the wrong choice not only once but twice.

7. You will also need to specify if you want dividends or capital gains to be reinvested to purchase more shares (usually at no additional cost to you) or flow to your money market / settlement fund. If you need the income, discussed later, select the money market / settlement fund. If you don't need the income and are in the process of building up the number of shares, select the Reinvest option.

Regardless of which option you select (cash or reinvest), if this transaction is held in a taxable account, the dividends will be considered as short-term *phantom income* and create a tax obligation. If qualified, the dividends may receive favorable tax treatment. It will be indicated on the 1099-B brokerage statement you will receive for tax filing purposes.

8. Periodically check the Order Status screen on the site to see if the order has executed or if it is still pending. You can usually alter the pricing that you would pay while in this screen if the security has jumped up in price from your original order's limit price and you just have to have it right away. Or you can walk away to have a cup of coffee and look at it later on. You'll usually end up paying more for the security if you look at the order screen too soon after placing the order and then get psyched into increasing your offer price.

9. The advice noted above for purchasing a security also applies for selling a security. Place the limit order and go about your business. If the security hits your limit specification, the trade will execute. Be very careful if you place your order to sell *at market*. Chances are the market price can drop, drastically at times, as the market makers (the people who facilitate the trade in the securities) see an opportunity to take you to the cleaners. Once executed, you're stuck with the final results, which can be financially painful.

10. When the order has executed, money to pay for any purchase will be debited from your money market fund / settlement account. When selling, your money market fund account will be credited with the proceeds.

How To Invest In Retirement

Investing during retirement will take some work and management on your part, but it can be made easier if you take your time and work closely with your advisor using the bucket approach. Divide your investments into three (3) buckets as follows:

Bucket 1. Ultrashort-term cash requirements should be held in money market funds, three- to five-year laddered CDs, and short-term bond mutual fund types of investments. This bucket includes your *financial gap* money needed within the next three to five years.

Bucket 2. Short- or mid-term should be composed of very low volatility investments including five-year laddered CDs, baby bonds with call features at least five years out, short-term bond mutual funds, and at the further end, balanced stock mutual funds, dividend mutual funds, etc. with low standard deviations. This bucket includes money needed within five to eight years and will also replenish the funds in Bucket 1 as they are withdrawn.

Bucket 3. This is your largest bucket of investments and is held long-term, where you can
consider varied stock mutual fund investments
(target date funds, large-cap index funds, nar-
rower-focused index funds, specialized funds,
MLPs, etc.) or zero-coupon bonds. This bucket
includes money that can be held for ten years or
longer and will be used to replenish the funds in
Bucket 2 as they are withdrawn.

Also see Morningstar's discussion of using a number of investment buckets for your retirement savings: https://www.morningstar.
com/articles/840177/the-bucket-approach-to-retirement-allocation.
html.

Tips And Financial Management Strategies During Your Retirement

I suggest you do not enter retirement carrying any large credit balances or even small ones. Mortgages, remodeling expenses, car loan payments, student loans, etc. should all be paid off before retiring, preferably at least one year prior to retiring, so you have time to actually see what your typical monthly expenses are going to be. Then you will need to make adjustments to them—additions for vacations and medical expenses, subtractions for commuting, business clothing, lunches eaten out, etc.

You'll likely find your grocery bill increasing as you'll probably eat at home more often and of better quality, and your medical expenses will generally increase each year as you age. Your auto costs and possibly your auto insurance costs should decrease. Inform your insurer when you retire so you can take advantage of less commuting mileage and road exposure, and take a senior driver's course every three years to save up to 10% on your policies. AARP offers courses online; AAA at their centers. I have taken both and prefer the in-person AAA course versus the online course.

Rebalance Your Investments At Least Once Annually

Reallocate into Buckets 1 and 2, moving from Buckets 2 and 3. Since mutual fund companies typically measure their performance January–December, use January as your annual rebalancing time.

Use a percentage method to keep your three investment buckets stocked up and within bounds.

The term "Sell in May and go away" is an old saying with fundamentally good reasons. Why? Tracking the market over the years, I see that people will fund their IRA contributions up through mid-April, just in time for filing their tax returns. They will usually place the money into their money market fund and then proceed to drive up the price of stocks / mutual funds during the latter part of April and early May when repositioning their money market investment. Once that happens and the monies have been invested, hawks swoop in and sell their shares, which are now priced higher, thus driving down or sideways the prices of stocks / mutual funds. That's been my observation over many years of watching the markets.

Do you remember discussing your $1 investment being only worth 89¢? During the summer, people are engaged in fun and games, so stocks tend to trade sideways or slide a bit, anticipating September and October, when people get interested in the markets once again. So buy in the first few months of the year and redirect your savings program into the money market over the summer months.

Accumulate money in your money market and come back in the late October, early November period to make your stock/fund purchases. Or wait until after mutual funds have made their distributions in early to mid-December to make any additional mutual fund purchases, especially in a taxable account. Or just wait until the beginning of January and start each year fresh.

Don't Run Out of Money before Your "Sell-By" Date Arrives

Retirement is not the time for you to have to consider cinching in your belt because your funds are getting low. Let's review ways to make your funds last throughout your retirement years. Also see https://www.foxbusiness.com/personal-finance/retirement-calculator-savings-money.

Drawing Down Your Investments

If you are healthy and have a family history of longevity, consider delaying taking the Social Security retirement benefits of the highest-earning spouse until the maximum age of 70 or close to it. From full retirement age (FRA) until age 70, your Social Security benefits increase approximately 8% each year.

Social Security benefits will last your lifetime (unless it runs out of money). If married, the larger-income earner may want to consider delaying taking their Social Security retirement benefits as long as possible, as the surviving spouse can move up to the deceased spouse's Social Security benefits amount when that time occurs, as long as the surviving spouse is over FRA.

I personally delayed taking my Social Security retirement benefits until I was 68, using our savings to carry us through to that point. See https://www.marketwatch.com/story/when-to-claim-social-security-how-long-will-you-live-2014-07-31.

Consider using the three (3) general investment buckets for your retirement, as previously discussed. Spread your investments between stocks, bonds, and cash equivalents.

Previous industry recommendations were to have 60% of your assets invested in stocks, with the balance in bonds and cash. With increasing longevity, the latest suggestion is to subtract your age from 115, and the resulting number is the percent that is recommended you have invested in stocks.

Use money market funds and five (5) five-year laddered CDs, with one CD maturing each year. Rebuild the money market funds and CDs with money siphoned from short-term/mid-term investments. Replenish those investments with money siphoned from the long-term investments. Look to rebalance at least once per year, preferably in early January.

Rule of thumb to make investments last a person's lifetime: withdraw no more than 4% the first year, then 4% plus the rate of inflation thereafter. Depending on the size of a person's investments, this may or may not meet the goal of lasting their lifetime. This was an earlier industry recommendation but has since shown that this may not work in 100% of the cases.

Another suggested method to ensure longevity of income is to draw from your investments according to the IRS RMD schedule. This schedule, available in IRS Publication 590, shows the table by age and the divisor to calculate against the total balance in your account as of December 31 of the preceding year.

A traditional approach to withdrawing income from your savings accounts in retirement has been to withdraw funds from one account at a time, beginning with your taxable account, then moving to your tax-deferred, and lastly to your tax-free account. The idea here is to let your tax-free accounts grow as long as possible.

However, according to an online article from Fidelity Investments, by using a *proportional* withdrawal strategy from all accounts, the income taxes can be better spread out over the life of the withdrawals. The proportional example from Fidelity illustrates an approximately 40% reduction in total paid-in income taxes versus using the traditional withdrawal approach.

Assumptions for the following table:

> Taxable account ($200,000), tax-deferred account ($250,000), and tax-free account ($50,000)
> 5% annual return, $25,000 annual gross Social Security retirement benefits
> Total after-tax income requirement need of $60,000 per year
> See https://www.fidelity.com/viewpoints/retirement /tax-savvy-withdrawals.

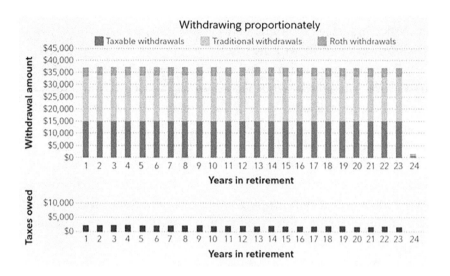

Another way to potentially ensure your income lasts through your retirement is, you could invest various amounts in a structured ladder of immediate annuities during your initial retirement years. Payout amounts from annuities change every time the Fed adjusts the funds rate, but let's use 6.5% as an example of an annual payout for a male aged 65 (females with expected longer lifetimes receive a bit less percentage amounts).

For a $100,000 investment, a retiree could expect to begin receiving $6,500 over the course of the year, paid monthly, for approximately $541 in income each month. $200,000 = $1,082, $300,000 = $1,623, and so on. Laddering the purchase of annuities could further serve to increase your expected monthly income with each new immediate annuity purchased.

Use only quality insurance companies and utilize more than one company if buying more than one annuity (i.e., don't invest all your annuity money with only one company). The maximum per insurance company is $100,000, but no more than that amount invested with any one company. Shop around.

State insurance administrators can help recover losses if a company goes out of business, but there is a limit to the amount of their coverage. Per company, $100,000 should be fine for ensuring your coverage in case of the insurer's bankruptcy. Check with your state insurance administrator to confirm their coverage amounts.

If you absolutely feel you have to invest in an annuity for your security and peace of mind during retirement, I suggest that you do not invest more than 40% of your retirement savings in immediate annuities; strive to limit your investment in immediate annuities to 30% or less of your savings. Be wary of advisors wanting to invest all or a majority of your savings in annuities. Run—or hobble—away!

How Much Immediate Income Will You Need?

To maintain your accustomed lifestyle, you will need at a minimum the difference between what you receive monthly from all sources (i.e., Social Security retirement benefits, other pension benefits, etc.) and what you pay out on your known recurring expenses. Plus, you will want to consider factoring in an inflation amount each year for cost-of-living increases. And this just covers your known amounts.

You should also allow for any unknown expenses that may suddenly and unexpectedly crop up (i.e., car repairs, water damage / broken pipes, roof repairs, and possibly medical conditions). One person I knew many years ago thought he'd retire with a small amount of savings in the bank. Shortly after, he needed a new roof on his home; he had to go back to work.

Personally, we walked into unplanned out-of-pocket medical expenses exceeding $30,000 the second year of our retirement. These items can be (and were by us) addressed with your emergency savings account (perhaps as part of your money market fund in your Roth IRA). Google Kiplinger's retirement savings calculator as well.

Annuity income will be fully taxable if drawn from a traditional/rollover IRA. If drawn from money that had already been taxed before you purchased the annuity, a portion of each payment will be considered as a return of principal, and the difference will be taxable. Only if paid from a fully qualified Roth IRA will the income from the annuity escape tax.

You can have the insurance company withhold an amount for taxes, or you can send in estimated tax payments on a quarterly basis to the IRS yourself using Form 1040-ES. Don't wait until tax filing time to pay your tax bill, or you will face stiff penalties for underpayment, plus interest.

Other ways to generate ongoing income would be interest from individual bond investments with lengthy maturity dates or dividend-paying stock or bond mutual funds. A retiree could draw the interest or dividends as the case may be and not touch the underlying investment. Over time, individual bonds will mature, and you will need to think about reinvesting the proceeds. But drawing the interest or the dividends and not touching the investment will continue to provide you with income as long as the company remains in business and hasn't cut, reduced, or stopped its quarterly dividend payments.

Long-Term Care Considerations

This book was written specifically for the average employee to educate and inform them of the various retirement savings plans available to them and the management of their investments in retirement. However, I would be remiss as a planner if I did not mention the need for reviewing and considering long-term care requirements.

Recognizing the possibility of requiring long-term care at some point in your life, more likely during your retirement, and how to handle the ever-rising costs of it is something that everyone should consider. Custodial care, skilled care, adult day health care (ADHC), and so on may be covered by Medicare for a limited number of days, but it comes with various qualifying requirements to obtain the coverage. If those qualifying requirements aren't met, you're pretty much left to your own resources. See https://www.medicareresources.org/faqs/to-what-extent-will-medicare-cover-long-term-care/.

In extreme financial hardship conditions, state Medicaid may step in to help with the costs. You've worked and saved all your life. Do you really want to become destitute to qualify for state Medicaid? And have you even seen or visited a state-supported long-term care facility?

This is where the benefits of long-term care insurance come into focus, supposing that you can

- qualify to obtain it and
- afford the premiums.

When applying for LTC insurance coverage, you'll have to fill out a questionnaire. If you've already been diagnosed with some illness or affliction, chances are that you will be disqualified from obtaining the coverage. Insurance companies are in business to make money, so they are highly restrictive in whom they will insure. If you're in great health, you're the one they want to enroll. If you're not in great health, not so much.

The marketplace for such insurance seems to be getting tighter all the time. Insurance companies that offered LTC insurance plans have gone through many phases. Some have gone out of business once the claims started coming in. Think about that—you paid your premiums for perhaps many years, and then you may be shut out of your full coverage. You're much older now, and you may be at the need point for assistance. But you can't qualify for another company's plan, and the costs if you do qualify are prohibitive. See https://www.penntreaty.com/Liquidation/LiquidationQuestions.aspx.

Other companies have dropped offering LTC insurance coverage altogether. There are some life insurance policies available that offer the ability to withdraw portions of the death benefits to help pay for long-term care if you have the right life insurance plan and cash value. See https://termlife2go.com/long-term-care-life-insurance/.

Or alternatively, you may self-pay if you are financially well-off.

There are book loads of statistics discussing the potential need or lack of need for LTC based on a person's age, health, lifestyle, if they are a couple and physically capable enough to assist one another, physically active, man's/woman's average length of stay in a facility if LTC is needed, etc. I'm not trying to scare you with this subject, but it needs to be examined before you find yourself in need.

The best advice I can offer in this book is to bring this issue to your foremost attention and to recommend that you consult with your financial advisor or an insurance agency offering LTC plans to discuss the means to handle your potential long-term care needs. Your employer may also offer an LTC plan for you and your family at relatively affordable rates. These are things that you should take into consideration and plan to handle should the need arise as the monthly/annual costs for LTC in a facility are high and increasingly higher each year.

My final comments on this issue is, check with an attorney specializing in elder care and estate planning, as laws change constantly, and what applies to people today for preservation of income and Medicaid eligibility may be totally different in another year or more.

Conclusion

The information I've presented to you here covers your basic retirement planning investment education. I have attempted to be as accurate as I could be in the descriptions and examples presented while making it interesting and involved. You should be much better educated now than you were before you picked up this book.

I encourage you to search online if you need deeper, fuller explanations. Certainly there is much more that you can and should learn about your investment plans, as no one will watch after your money better than you will. Hopefully, this short, concise book has given you the push in the direction you needed to get started on your plan for your future wealth and financial well-being.

I suggest that you keep this book handy near your computer so you can quickly locate and reread topics as they present themselves while reviewing your investment plans. You should now be confident in your knowledge and well-informed on the general basics of investing in the assortment of retirement plans that are available to you and their many "gotcha" tax implications.

Your next step is to meet with a professional to help generate your retirement investment portfolio or help guide you if you DIY. Look for professionals with CFP® and EA credentials, CPAs that work with and advise on mutual funds, and/or attorneys in the investment business with master tax training. You will want to work with a fiduciary that is familiar with the tax consequences of the investments.

You don't want to invest in something only to have to give it all up to taxes. Take your time and qualify your investment advisor.

Thank you for purchasing and reading my book. I sincerely hope it helps to bring you much financial peace of mind and an enjoyable retirement in the years to come. Good luck to you and your future.

> *Experience* is what you get when you don't listen
> to knowledgeable advice. (Author unknown)

Important Legal Documents

I've added this page since you'll be doing so well with your investing that you'll want to specify to whom and how much to leave it to or how to spend it on you when you can't decide for yourself.

Almost everyone has heard that they should have a will that's properly drafted by an attorney, signed, and witnessed. A will is a legal document necessary for the distribution of your assets upon passing if not specified by contract or other legal document taking precedence elsewhere. A will is also where you can identify and designate guardians for your surviving minor children.

Probate is the legal process used to distribute a deceased person's estate to heirs and ensure debtors are properly paid. Beneficiary forms in your IRAs and 401(k)s operate as a matter of contract, maintain privacy, and are processed outside of probate and the will. Trusts also operate outside of probate and maintain privacy.

But is a will and contracts for disposition of your estate all that you need?

In a word, no! There are several additional legal documents that you should have arranged and ready to go in case of need. Briefly, I will identify them here. These items should be consulted with, drafted, and executed by an attorney competent in estate planning and senior care needs.

1. A *medical directive*, also known as a *living will* or *advanced health-care directive*—these are instructions for your care

when you are personally unable to instruct the medical professionals.

2. A *durable power of attorney for health-care and HIPAA release*—this permits your designees to make the health-care decisions for you and gives them access to your medical records and to discuss your condition with the medical professionals.

3. A *durable power of attorney for finances*—this appoints your designee to handle financial transactions for you while you are unable to do so.

4. Maybe a *revocable living trust*—this allows you to control your estate while living and identifies to whom the trust will distribute estate property according to your wishes once you've passed on. This document and the properties contained therein also avoid probate. Note: Property must be titled to the trust to be effective. Creating a trust does nothing if it is not funded.

5. A *will*.

Notice that the will is the last item in this list. The items preceding it are just as important for the well-being of a person still living and those responsible for their care. Paraphrasing Dave Ramsey, "obtaining these documents is the adult thing to do."

Additional Resources

I have read each of the books listed on this page and highly recommend them to you. I have also used the online references as noted, in addition to reading scores of other books on topic over the years. And of course, the continuous study for my professional licensing and the many years of personal experience both saving for and then within retirement are all built into the knowledge transfer I have provided to you in this book.

- *You Can Retire Sooner Than You Think* by Wes Moss, CFP®. This book lays out one of the most perfect and simplistic investment plans for retirement. Why make yourself crazy? This is the book that I should have written. The only additional chapter that I feel should have been written and included in this book, but wasn't, is how to pay off your mortgage in half the time, even if it is a fifteen-year mortgage (and assuming your mortgage contract permits early principal repayment). Otherwise, it is a perfect "how to and in what to invest" bookend mate to my book. It was endorsed by radio host Clark Howard too. If you don't read any other book listed here, read this one.
- *The Truth About Money* by Ric Edelman. An excellent resource for general financial planning purposes. The only point in the entire book with which I disagree is the recommendation to carry a mortgage in retirement for cap-

ital "leverage" to improve one's financial position. Ric is much younger than me. *Not during retirement!* Do you really want to lay awake at night thinking about making the next mortgage payment? Think SWAN and have pleasant dreams.

- Financial books by Suze Orman, CFP®. All her many books that I have read are on target.
- Online information on IRAs, Roth IRAs, 401(k)s, and Roth 401(k)s by Ed Slott, CPA. Ed is *the* go-to guru regarding these subjects, but always check other resources as well as things change.
- PBS TV programming on retirement savings by Ed Slott, CPA. Ed appears frequently on PBS and has developed several books available to you only by making a donation to PBS. I feel that this is an excellent financial educational opportunity and a worthwhile charitable cause.
- *Die Broke* by Stephen Pollan, JD, and Mark Levine. The authors advise loading up on annuities.
- *Don't Die Broke* by David J. Reindel. This book takes a slightly different approach to the *Die Broke* position. Both are worth reading and considering for your personal courses of action.
- *How to Retire Happy, Wild, and Free* by Ernie J. Zelinski. This book explores everything but money in the pursuit of your enjoyment in the retirement years. Highly recommended.
- Online investing resources available through the following:
- TD Ameritrade, Charles Schwab, Fidelity, Vanguard, T. Rowe Price, Kiplinger.com, Morningstar
- www.usatoday.com/story/money/columnist/waggoner/2013/08/15/target-date-retirement-funds/2661691/
- www.troweprice.com/personal-investing/mutual-funds/target-date-funds.html

- www.investopedia.com/terms/a/annualized-total-return.asp
- https://www.daveramsey.com/
- https://clark.com/

APPENDIX A

APPENDIX A: Sample 401(K) Plan Allocation

Below is an example of a suggested 401(k) savings plan discussed with a 54-year-old former colleague planning to continue working in their management position until age 66 or 67 and contributing to their plan with each paycheck. The colleague presented the information to me with the investment options available in their plan and their current allocation as shown.

I reviewed the performance of the investments online and created three adjustments for the colleague to consider making an immediate readjustment using the current funds in the account and the new paycheck contributions, then another adjustment at age 56 applying only to the new contributions, and a third and final adjustment at age 62, again applying only to the new contributions.

Performance as of December 31, 2018—Funds listed have recovered all losses and have gained positively at the time of this writing.

Fund	Current	Performance			*Adjust Now	Age 56–62	Age 62–66/67
Selections	Allocation	1 year	3 year	5 year		Future Alloc	Future Alloc
Retire Trust	5.96%	2.0%	6.8%	4.1%	15%	25%	15% or 20%
Target 2025	1.37%	–5.3%	6.59%	5.09%	0%	0%	0%
Target 2030	0%	–6.04%	6.85%	5.27%	5%	5%	5% or 0%
Int'l Stock	0.35%	–14.4%	4.48%	6.30%	0%	0%	0%
Small-Cap	4.01%	–9.43%	7.51%	5.12%	0%	0%	0%
Mid-Cap	20.78%	–9.24%	6.39%	6.22%	0%	0%	0%
Index 500	9.7%	–4.42%	9.22%	8.46%	75%	50%	10%
Bond	0%	3.49%	1.9%	2.32%	0%	15%	40%
Stable Value	57.83%	2.25%	1.97%	1.88%	5%	5%	30%
Total	100%				100%	100%	100%

*Then change future contributions as shown for the age periods indicated.

After readjusting the existing investments per the Adjust Now column, do not further change the existing investments. This will ensure sufficient stock accumulation for the retirement years while building up cash and bonds in the period between age 56 and retirement. Then just before retirement, the portfolio will need to be reviewed and adjustments made to the investment mix to fit the colleague's requirements during retirement and to prepare for rollout to their IRA.

Notes on the investment selections:

The Retirement Trust fund is allocated 60% bond / 40% stock.

The Target Date Trust funds begin their *retirement* year with approximately 90% in stocks and slide to approximately 20% stock / 80% bonds *over a thirty-five year period*.

Because of the Target's lengthy period to reach its most conservative position, the colleague is better off using the Retirement Trust fund for its more conservative 60% bond / 40% stock allocation, coupled with a sizeable position in the Index 500 fund (which tapers off, percentagewise, of the total gross portfolio over time).

After seven years, compare the returns of the 2030 Target Date Trust fund to the Retirement Trust fund to determine the next five-plus years of investments in the plan. If appropriate, swap future investment direction and total balance at that time from the 2030 Target Date Trust fund to the Retirement Trust fund.

The Index 500 fund includes both Small-Caps and Mid-Caps, so there is no need to separately invest in them, and on the plus side, it reduces the standard deviation. American companies, included in the Index 500 fund, have enough international exposure. Based on many years of underperformance, I do not see any reason to invest directly in an international fund.

Reallocate the current cash amount now by shuffling the funds as noted.

The Retirement Trust, with its 60% allocation to bonds, enables a lower direct Bond fund allocation.

Build cash (Stable Value) and bonds over the next ten to twelve years.

Build a large cash/bond position during the final working years to fund the short-term bucket of cash, laddered CDs, baby bonds, etc. upon retirement.

SWAN.

APPENDIX B

These are the categories I have been tracking for many years leading to and then in retirement. The left column of the spreadsheet lists all the categories listed below and includes an average amount per each item that is anticipated to be paid. The actual data is inserted per line in twelve monthly columns as it is spent, with a summary column of the year's activity on the right side and a final column next to the summary illustrating the anticipated spend versus the actual spend.

Knowing your sources of income and expense categories will help you manage and control your finances both before and during retirement. If you don't know your expenses going into retirement, how on earth will you know how much income you will need in retirement?

INCOME
(Two or three line entries covering all income sources)
Total

EXPENSES
Annual Fixed Expenses

110

(Sam's Club, AARP, AAA, property tax, car tags, professional licenses, education, Amazon, A/C service, social clubs, PC antivirus, RMD, and income taxes)
Total

Monthly Fixed Expenses
(Medical insurance, vehicle/home insurance, fitness club, pest control, electric, phone, utilities, cell, life insurance, lawn service, pool service)
Total

Monthly Variable Expenses (This category gets adjusted based on available income.)
(Groceries, gasoline, cash, restaurants, vitamins, donations, medical copays, vehicle repairs, house repairs, clothing, haircuts/salon, magazines, pool supplies, entertainment, gifts, vacations, miscellaneous. If it doesn't fall into one of the defined categories, it goes in the miscellaneous line.)
Total

Total Monthly Expenses (Summation of all the above.)

Estimated Excess Income (Arrived after subtracting expenses from income. Result goes to savings.)

Savings (Preretirement, pay yourself first by populating savings before tackling other expenses. Adjust what you spend in the monthly variable expenses as required.)

About the Author

After fifty years of full-time employment in military, government, corporate, and private environments, Ed retired in March 2015. His last corporate business experience was spent working as a principal contracts negotiator with Symantec Corp., a major software corporation, for twelve years. Prior to that, Ed worked in contracts administration, vendor management, and mainframe systems engineering for AT&T for over nineteen years and as a software developer for Johnson & Johnson and the US government for a combined four years.

Ed's military background included over ten years of active duty in infantry and computer programming assignments (1966–76), predominantly in Germany, where he was assigned for over seven years. Ed spent a year in combat as a member of a rifle company in the First Infantry Division in Vietnam (1967–68), where he was awarded two Purple Heart medals for wounds and the Combat Infantryman Badge.

After leaving active duty, Ed joined the Army Reserves where he served for more than eleven years (1976–88), attaining the rank of Master Sergeant. While in the Reserves, Ed served as a paratrooper in a Special Ops unit, was a senior Drill Sergeant at Fort Dix, New Jersey, served as a senior instructor in the NCO Academy, and was a systems analyst at First Army headquarters at Fort Meade, Maryland.

Educationally, Ed was on the honor and merit rolls in high school, leaving in the eleventh grade to join the Army. He subsequently obtained his GED and began attending college at night while in the military. Ed went on to graduate in '79 from Rutgers University with a bachelor of arts degree, carrying a full-time academic load at night while working his full-time day job with overtime requirements and weekend military reserve duties. Ed is fluent in German and dabbles in French and Italian.

Not fully understanding the investments available to him through his company's 401(k) plan in the early '90s, Ed enrolled in several investment and tax courses and, eventually, the Certified Financial Planner™ course at Rollins College. He then pursued his master of business administration degree with a concentration in finance from Webster University, following which Ed attended Barry University School of Law.

Professional designations: He passed the prestigious CFP® exam in '96, then self-studied and passed the Enrolled Agent exam with the IRS in 2002. Prior to taking the EA exam, Ed self-studied and passed the SEC Series 7 exams.

Ed has worked in the financial management planning and tax return preparation field as an individual practitioner in his own business. His private practice concentrated on tax return preparation and the aspects of taxation in personal financial management and retirement investment planning.

Since retiring from the corporate technology world, Ed has maintained his professional designations by taking required annual continuing education courses, working gratis with individuals, and writing. This is Ed's first book on retirement investment preparation and tax strategy planning.

Ed and his wife, Sue, also a Rutgers University graduate (BS degree in computer science), have been together thirty-nine years and counting. They enjoy traveling, cooking, reading, movies, and exercise.

CPSIA information can be obtained
at www.ICGtesting.com
Printed in the USA
FSHW021641180720